PENRIN BOYS

FREDERICK W. PENNEY

A Pennco Publishing Book

*This book is dedicated to
Frederick E. Penney Jr.
who figured out that the country was
what was best for his boys.*

The Penryn Boys
Copyright © 2009 by Pennco Publishing & Frederick W. Penney.
All rights reserved.

Publisher: Pennco Publishing
Editor: Mark Hayward
Cover: Keith Brown
Typography: LB Designs.

First Edition: October 2009

Printed in the United States of America.

❧ TABLE OF CONTENTS ❧

THE PENRYN BOYS
❧ SUMMER OF '73 ❧
PROLOGUE

In 1864 a man by the name of Griffith Griffith came from a town in Wales called Penhryn and moved to what was then a wilderness area near Smithville (Loomis), California. Griffith bought some property from the Southern Pacific Railroad near English Colony for what would be the first Granite Quarry in the area. Soon, many ranchers, miners, and farmers would move into the area to use the newly discovered rich granite soils deposits of ore in English Colony, now renamed Penryn. Also, the fruit and cattle industry began to flourish by the 1890's.

Gold mines began popping up all around Placer County in the 1800's, and many prospectors came looking to strike it rich in the hills of Penryn. Many of these mines were bored right through the side of a mountain, usually right near a fruit orchard or cattle ranch. However, as the times changed many

1

of the mines were abandoned and left to fall apart by the gold seeking miners. Many of the mines were in areas that were thick with trees, vines and grasses. Eventually the entrance to these dangerous mines would be covered by thick wild vines, trees and bushes. Their deep shafts would slowly fill with spring water bubbling up slowly in a number of the tunnels. Soon, no one would know where the mines were located except through some old records kept at the county concerning the locations of each mine. Many of these abandoned mines were not even recorded with the county and sat unknown, hidden, and abandoned long ago.

These abandoned gold mines were difficult to find and often sat undiscovered for years until someone stumbled upon them by accident. After I moved to Penryn as a child, I heard of a mine rumored to exist in the area called the Bickford Mine. This was one of the many deep, dark, hidden mines that only a few local people knew existed in Penryn. Mothers worried about their children falling down a deep shaft of one of these abandoned mines. Rumors swirled around all the local schools of men and women being murdered and their bodies tossed down abandoned mines. Kids and adults alike talked about the spirits and ghosts that visited the mines, still trying to strike it rich even after the mines were stripped of their gold.

Bickford Ranch was a large 2000 acre ranch that took up a large portion of the area around Penryn. The ranch straddled the Southern Pacific Railroad land that ran directly through the ranch toward the great Sierra Nevada Mountain Range. Some of the best cattle in the valley grazed the tender grass of the rolling oak-studded hills. As a young man I never thought of the potential of this land becoming anything but a large cattle ranch for the Bickford family.

As time crawled on, the Penryn area farmers and ranchers began to disappear. By the 1960's many of the cattle ranches were gone and only a few select ones stayed, with the owners barely making a living and trying to resist the temptation of selling to big land companies who wanted to bring a larger population to the beautiful rolling hills of Penryn. The small fruit orchards had brought money and people to the small town of Penryn. These orchards of Penryn were more productive than those of other areas because they yielded more of a crop with a smaller plot of land. However, the orchards began to disappear as did the ranches as the land was sold off.

As Sacramento, California began to expand farther out toward the country, my father, Frederick Nickel Jr., began to worry that the urban sprawl might affect his boys. Father had a rough upbringing and did not want his boys to endure the same hardships that he had to go through. Father was the son of a single mother that had a drinking problem. He would spend many nights as a very young child sleeping in a car out in front of a bar. By the age of fourteen he was out of the house, living with relatives in Lake County, California. By the age of seventeen, Father was getting into trouble and decided that he would enlist in the Marines to keep himself out of trouble. Before Father knew it, he was fighting on the front lines in Korea, carrying a machine gun up ahead of everyone else. He told many stories in his later years about how he was one of the main night scouts that would sneak around the jungle to find the enemy camps. His two serious wounds from the war eventually took his life when his boys were still very young adults. When we were little, his strong belief was that country life did boys good and hard ranch work made boys into men. Mom believed that Dad had a jaded take on living in the country. She fought him to the end to stay in the city with her boys. However, Father prevailed, bringing with the family and his in-laws, Floyd and Myrna Davis.

In the late 1960's and early 1970's the population of Penryn, California was slowly growing to where it was reaching close to 700 people. Most of the people in town and at the ranches were migrant workers picking and packing fruit. There were fruit packing sheds all over the area with a steady stream of laborers coming from all over the country to find seasonal work. The neighboring towns of Loomis and Newcastle were bustling during the summer with the fruit trucks driving around the towns loaded down with the fresh crop from their fields to the Blue Anchor and High Hand fruit packing sheds next to the railroad tracks. This was an exciting time as all the children were out of school, and most of them were working on a fruit ranch or at the packing sheds. The few cattle ranches that still existed employed the toughest of the kids from school who could wrestle a cow or two. You could always tell these young men in town with their straw cowboy hats and pointed cowboy boots. They rarely took the time to hang out with anyone else other than their own type.

Everybody knew each other in Penryn. The local watering hole next to Moto's Market was the main social hangout in town. The population of Penryn was made up of a fair number of Japanese

Americans, many of whom were the very individuals that were put in detention camps during World War II. Many of the farms in Penryn were owned by Japanese families that had lived in the area for decades. You could see the old Japanese farmers sitting on the front porch of the local watering hole, their own front porches, or at Moto's market just in town. They would just sit and pass the time away talking about the good old days. They were past their time and probably felt that their great depth of knowledge of farming and how to grow beautiful sweet fruit were no longer needed. The slow paced, simple life was slowly leaving Penryn (and Loomis), and city people were just starting to learn of the area and move in. The Nickel boys were part of that unwanted crowd that brought their fast paced city ways with them. At least that was what the locals believed and they could not be told otherwise.

Penryn was in a transition stage at the time the Nickel boys moved to their small ranch in the early 1970s. Moto's market would see new customers that did not speak Japanese and that did not want to walk next to the large fish counter with octopus and squid as the main selling item. The small town was in for a change: the busy-body out-of-town Nickel boys were moving in and all hell was about to break loose.

CHAPTER ONE
THE CARPETBAGGERS

June 1973

The Nickel family stood out like a sore thumb the first day we came to Penryn, at the start of summer vacation in 1973, and not just because of the car. Granted, it was only three years old, wasn't leaking oil, and had all of its hubcaps, but that was not our family's only oddity. Simply put, we were city folk, which was plain enough to see when you saw the matriarch of the family. Mom was tall and slender, and the house she had kept in Sacramento was as immaculate as her perfectly manicured fingernails. Her eyes became wider and wider with each house we drove by, as barnyard animals, rusted Fords, and dirty barefoot children composed a picture quite different from the Norman Rockwell scene she had envisioned. Two particular specimens were giving each other mud baths in front of their shambling house. Mom groaned, and

7

I heard her mutter a desperate prayer.

Dad at least looked the part more than Mom did. Even though he was in his forties, Dad could never find a shirt that fit his bulging biceps. He had been a cop and was a former Marine who had fought the Communists hand-to-hand in Korea, and he made sure that everyone saw the large Marine First Division tattoo on his right shoulder and arm. Hippie protesters usually shut up pretty quickly when Dad growled down at them. He had a vein that popped out of his forehead when he got mad, and that was usually enough to get them to mutter something about "supporting the troops, just not the cause" and scurry away. I knew that look, too, and was smart enough to run when I saw it. He was actually kind of a softie deep down, but we made sure not to let on that we knew it. Dad would do just fine in the backwoods, and he also believed that old fashioned country values and the American work ethic would do more for his sons than what he perceived as the "liberal educations" we were getting at the hands of the teachers' union in the big city. Dad wanted us to go to an old fashioned country school, one where the principal used the paddle often and ran the school like a Marine drill sergeant.

That was fine by us…well, not the work ethic part, but our humble new home looked a lot more exciting than any of the suburbs we had lived in. I hated reading for school, but I was a big fan of Louis L'Amour, and the landscape around me looked like one of his novels come to life. We had left the freeway and were driving on an old cement highway patched with asphalt every few feet. We saw birds, beautiful gray California quail, running along the road in front of us. They acted like they were daring my father to run them over, and Dad took them up on the offer. Dad wasn't the type to stop for a bird, and the birds apparently weren't all that bright, because our fender was covered in feathers when we later stopped. The frequent potholes jolted the Dodge Dart station wagon. David and I grinned, using the jostling as an excuse to start smashing Floyd between us every time the car hit a hole and we took a hit. He knew better than to complain, and tried dishing back, but we were bigger and stronger and he could do nothing to stop us

We crossed some railroad tracks and turned east, and David and I gave up bumping Floyd to look out the window. Soon we were at Grandma and Grandpa Davis's ranch, which was right next to our new ranch. The car came to a gradual stop, dust billowing up from the back of the car. We had been cooped up in the car for way too long, and as soon as Dad braked we were out the doors.

We bolted through Grandma and Grandpa Davis's thick overgrown field, ignoring Mom's shouts to come back and greet our grandparents. We knew them and could see them anytime, but this field was ripe to explore. Grandma and Grandpa's property used to be a large thriving plum farm. In between the former Japanese owner being removed to an internment camp during World War II and Grandpa Davis' purchase of the land, the field had degenerated into wild lands filled with animals and birds of all kinds. Dad had even told us that there were mountain lions and rattlesnakes in the area. He told us that very sternly, emphasizing that we were under no circumstances to look for or try to catch such dangerous predators. We had nodded solemnly while our imaginations conjured up a great lion or snake hunt. We were young Davy Crocketts and this was our wild frontier. No lions dared to show themselves that day, but there was plenty of smaller game that welcomed us to Penryn.

There were four of us. Floyd was the youngest of the Nickel boys, a short, stocky, eight-year-old blue-eyed blonde boy who had an even higher voice than most kids his age. Sometimes we called him "Racing Stripe" since he hated changing his white cotton briefs, which left him with a notorious brown stripe from days or even weeks of use. Stubbornness, of course, is a family trait learned and inherited from Dad's side of the family. David was eleven years old and chubby. We called him "Stoopy" because he was kind of—well, stupid. Maybe a kinder explanation would be that he lacked common sense. Every thing he touched broke, every thing he was assigned to clean ended up dirtier when he was done, and every argument he was ever in ended up with him losing and in frustration yelling "No, you're stupid!" Then there was Scott, who, at fifteen, was the oldest. He was actually smart, and, unlike most of us, had a lot of patience. He must have gotten it from Mom. Occasionally, though, Dad's temper came out in him. It didn't happen a lot, but when Scott got mad, you didn't want to get in the way. In fact, it was easy to tell that he was starting to lose it when white, foamy spit started to form around the corners of his mouth. Floyd once ended up in hysterics when his favorite teddy bear ended up in Scott's rampage path. Scott felt awful after, and used his savings to replace the newly-decapitated stuffed animal. Of course, it was kind of ironic that Floyd was upset as his favorite thing to do was to play with army men, killing each of the enemy with a kitchen knife and on occasion decapitating the enemy soldier.

My name is Fred, and most people called me "Freddie" in 1973. They also used to call me "Fast Freddie" because I was always on the go. My teachers called me other things because I was always on the go during their classes, but this is my story and I don't have to share what they thought. I was thirteen years old in 1973.

"Boys, get back here!" Dad's voice cut through the field. We knew that tone of voice, and reluctantly gave up chasing a pheasant to return to the car. Dad gave Scott a gentle swat upside the head. David sniggered, so he got one, too, that wasn't quite as gentle. I knew to keep my mockery hidden, so I stayed quiet. Mom set us to work, lugging our stuff into Grandma and Grandpa's mostly finished house. Our house wasn't quite finished yet, so we were staying with Grandma and Grandpa until ours was ready for us to move in.

Grandpa was there at the car, helping Mom with her huge suitcase. When he saw us, he put it down and gave us each a huge bear hug. "How are ya, my boys?" he boomed, looming over us. "Glad to be out of the city?"

"Yes, sir," we replied in unison. "Huge" was the word that went through anyone's mind the first time they met Grandpa. Well, huge and bald, but he was huge enough that most people didn't mention the hair loss. My dad was a big guy, but Grandpa's huge arms made Dad's look like pencils. Grandpa had grown up in the backwoods of Idaho, and after a life spent in the city, he had finally talked our city-loving Grandma into moving to Penryn. I hadn't seen him since they left Sacramento, and the change was obviously agreeing with him. He exuded vigor in his faded pair of overalls, plaid shirt, and new straw cowboy hat.

"You boys ready for some adventures?" he asked. "We've got some great stuff picked out for you...."

"Floyd!" a loud voice barked from the porch. "Stop holding everyone up and get those things in the house!"

"Yes, dear," he called back. "If I didn't love that woman so much, I'd kick her butt," he growled much more softly, shooting us a wink as he stooped to pick up Mom's suitcase. We laughed, but knew not to let Grandma hear us either.

If country life was agreeing with Grandpa, it looked pretty obvious that Grandma was still trying to assert some of her high-society Southern California upbringing in Penryn. Her perfectly coiffed shoulder-length auburn hair still didn't show any gray. Her back stayed ramrod straight when she hugged us, even when she had to stoop down to hug Floyd. Just like always, she had a batch of her fresh-baked peanut butter chocolate chip cookies ready for us, so we attacked those as she asked us about the drive up from Sacramento.

My grandparents' story is very interesting. Grandma's parents were pretty high up in Los Angeles society: Her dad had been a big something-or-other and her mother had won some beauty pageant back in the 1920s. "Stuffed shirts" was what Grandpa called them, and it was still a miracle that this high society girl had married an Idaho farm boy. Rumor had it that Grandma had a tall, dark and handsome city boy that fancied her. I wasn't sure what "fancied" meant then, but Grandma and Grandpa always used those kinds of words. I assumed it meant that he liked her. Grandma always talked about that man as if it was her first and only love, but Grandpa was in the picture back then and would have nothing to do with it. In Idaho the Davis boys had the reputations of being the town bullies, and Grandpa kept that reputation alive wherever he lived. Mom once told me that this old boyfriend of Grandma's had been on the way back from college to propose when Grandpa met him at the train station and let him know exactly what would happen to him if he stepped off the train. Well, the fellow wisely decided to keep on going, and Grandpa proposed that night, supposedly using the same roses that the city slicker had dropped at the train station.

Even though their marriage had started out with a little bit of mischief on Grandpa's part, he was always the gentleman to her. He stayed in Los Angeles and Sacramento even though the country was in his blood. In fact, it's still a miracle to me how he finally convinced Grandma to move out to the country. The move hadn't been easy for Grandma, and the inside of the new ranch house still looked as opulent as their old place in Sacramento. "Pardon the mess and the dust," she apologized time and time again, despite the fact that the house was nearly spotless.

It was getting dark when we finally unpacked, so we were forced to stay inside for the evening. Scott and I ended up in the back spare bedroom, and he was nice enough to take the sleeping bag and give me the bed. Across the hall, we heard Mom separating David and Floyd from another fight. Our room faced Grandma and Grandpa's pond, which was fed by a rippling brook. The window was open, and I pulled the covers close to my neck to ward off the cool evening breeze. The sound of the water cascading over the rocks from out front was soothing and caused me to instantly relax. I started to drift asleep as the gentle rippling of the brook drowned out the heated sounds from the living room. Grandma and Dad were playing cards, and Dad was accusing Grandma of cheating again. She probably had been: Grandma couldn't stand losing at anything, especially to my father. A smile slowly formed on my face, which shifted to a contented yawn as I drifted off to sleep.

CHAPTER TWO
PLUMBALL

The next morning dawned bright and clear, and the four Nickel boys slipped quickly away from the house to the large and spacious green field. Saturday usually meant lots of chores in our household, but not on Grandma's watch. "You boys go explore tomorrow," she had urged us the night before. "Just make sure you're gone early before your mean Grandpa and Dad make you boys spend the day working."

"What was that?" Grandpa had yelled from the bridge table, sourly eyeing his cards.

We heeded Grandma's advice and ran out as soon as the sun was up. Grandma and Grandpa's house sat on the edge of a beautiful small brook that cascaded down a five-foot waterfall from the east side of their property. We ran to where it ended in a small pond that was filled with blue gill that Grandpa caught down at the Sadlers' large lake that lay just over the hill from Grandpa's ranch. Several mallards also lived on the pond. David tried to make a grab for a little duckling, but the mother quickly swooped in on him. David yelped when she nipped his hand, which naturally made the rest of us burst out laughing.

"Shut up," David whined, sucking on his hand. "You couldn't do any better."

"You got beat up by a duck!" Floyd scoffed in his high pre-puberty voice.

"C'mon, idiots," Scott chuckled. "We're still right next to the house. Let's go find something cooler."

"Yeah," I seconded. "David could get beaten up by the duck again and get injured."

David threw a half-hearted punch at me as he jogged by, but there was too much to see to linger over the ducks for too long anyway. Soon we came across two large plum trees left over from the old Japanese farm. They were heavily laden. One plum tree had dark purple plumbs that were almost as big as baseballs. The other tree was loaded with small, ripe yellow plums that were almost all uniformly the size of a golf ball. David, still grumbling from the duck incident, grabbed one and chucked it against the wall of Grandpa's newly painted chicken coup. It splattered, leaving a juicy red and purple stain. Scott and I whistled in admiration. David grinned, and then all three of us looked at Floyd, who was obliviously pulling up dirt a few yards away. We each got the same brilliant idea. Soon, Floyd was yelping as he tried to dodge dozens of incoming plums. His skin and clothing were red, purple and yellow by the time we were done.

"Stop!" he whimpered.

We let up after at least a few more throws each. "Make sure you wash your underwear when you wash everything else," I advised, patting him on the head. He wasn't particularly amused.

Bored after a few minutes, we began to explore the southern part of the property. We found an old barbed wire fence behind Grandma and Grandpa's field. We could see that the neighbors herded sheep. The many holes in the fence attested to the sheep's stupidity, as did the blood on the barbed wire. Scott tried his aim with the plums at one of the sheep and was rewarded with a loud "Baa!" and a nice red and purple stain on the sheep's white fluff. Above the hill on the neighbors' property, I noticed a huge granite boulder that looked like a mushroom. It looked a lot like one on my grandparents' property, but I noticed something moving around this one. It didn't look like a sheep. I quickly dropped to my knees, hiding in the tall grass while my brothers kept playing. A small boy was hiding behind the rock, watching my brothers play. He was wearing overalls and a red T-shirt and looked to be around David's age.

I noticed a few scattered plums by my feet from other old plum trees near the fence line, and a malicious smile slowly spread over my face. I scooped one up. The boy had still not seen me, and his attention was riveted on my brothers. I had a good arm from my time on the Cubs, my Little League team in Sacramento, and I cocked my arm and let the plum fly. My aim wasn't perfect, but I managed to splat the plum on the rock just a few inches away from his face. He let out a surprised yelp and ducked out of sight.

My brothers heard the yell and turned from their game. "Quick," I hissed, motioning them to get down. "We've got a spy." They grinned and dropped into the tall grass, grabbing for ammunition. We waited, and soon we saw the spy's mussed brown hair poking up over the top of the rock. "FIRE!" I yelled, and we let our ammunition fly. He ducked quickly again as we threw plum after plum. Soon almost the entire rock was covered in plum juice, and the boy was nowhere to be seen.

"Serves you right!" I yelled, and my brothers and I congregated to congratulate each other on our victory. Just then, a rock whizzed right between Scott and me. Another one right behind it hit David in the right shoulder. He cried out in pain, while going down.

"Everyone down!" Scott yelled, pushing Floyd into the tall grass. I followed as more rocks flew around us. "David, you all right?" he asked.

David nodded. His shoulder wasn't bleeding or anything, but he already had a nice welt forming up. "This kid means business."

"He has started war against the Nickel boys." I said grimly. Our enemy might be Warren Spahn for all we knew, but there were four of us, and you didn't mess with the Nickel boys. We huddled with all the seriousness of a council of war. Scott quickly devised a plan. We reloaded with plums and broke off. David and I snuck carefully through the barbed wire, while Scott and Floyd kept the boy's attention with their own barrage. Plums and rocks flew back and forth as we carefully maneuvered around the sheep. Our goal was to hem him in on both sides, trap him, and then give him the plum-throwing beatdown of his life.

I reached my side before David reached his. Battle rage was coursing through my veins, and waiting was no longer an option for me. With my back to the rock, I slowly inched around the corner. I whirled into my position, my arm cocked to throw…but our enemy was gone!

I felt a tap on my shoulder and turned. The boy stood in front of me with a big smile on his face. "How did you…how did you do that?" I stammered in amazement.

He shrugged. "I'm quick," he answered. My brothers clambered up next to me. The boy eyed them warily, noticing the plums in their hands. I eyed the boy up and down and noticed not one bit of plumb juice on him; we had obviously missed with every shot. At first I thought he was a younger boy, but it was now obvious that he was much older than David but very short. He straightened and cracked a slight smile. "My name's Dwayne," he offered tentatively, extending his hand.

That was enough to force a truce. "Freddie," I answered, shaking it firmly with a plum-stained hand. My brothers came up and introduced themselves, and pretty soon we were fast friends.

Dwayne went on to tell us that he was fourteen and had lived here all his life, tending sheep and playing baseball at the local country field. He said that he also loved to explore the vast fields and hills that stretched throughout Penryn.

Grandpa interrupted our new venture—a game that we named Plumball, which was basically plum fights with teams—around noon to haul us back for chores. We looked around for Dwayne, but he had slipped off as soon as he heard Grandpa's voice. Grimly, we dropped our remaining plums and resigned ourselves to our fates. After scolding us for our appearance and forcing us into the tub, he put us to work cleaning the garage and dirty poop-filled chicken coop. That was not a good way to spend a Saturday, and we were all out of sorts by the time the cleaning was finally over.

After dinner, Scott and I went outside to sit on the porch. We were tired, and I was just starting to drift off when a plum splatted right at my feet. "Gotcha!" a high voice sounded from the dark yard. Scott and I looked at each other, grinned, and bounded into the darkness to chase our new friend.

CHAPTER THREE
OLD MAN SHEPMAN

We were back in Penryn the next weekend. Our little thousand square foot house in Sacramento had seemed smaller after the weekend in the country, and we spent the week counting the days until we could be back in Penryn. Dwayne was standing with Grandma and Grandpa to meet us when the pea green 1968 Dodge Corona station wagon pulled up. Grandma didn't look too thrilled about the dirty Penryn boy dragging us off again this weekend, but she still managed to smile when she saw us. She even gave Dwayne a cookie, which we took to be a good omen.

After a reprise of Plumball on Friday night, we were ready for something different on Saturday. Dwayne took charge and led us through the rolling hills and granite outcroppings that stretched for miles beyond his parents' property. Despite his small size, he was actually older than I, so he walked in front with Scott and me while David and Floyd tagged along behind us.

It was around noon, and Floyd and David had veered off to try to catch a pair of chipmunks. Dwayne was amused and followed behind them. Scott hung back, and I noticed that he didn't look too interested. *Come to think of it,* I thought, *he hasn't been too excited about anything since we left Sacramento.* I stayed back a little bit with him. "Hey bud, you okay?" I asked.

Scott started. He'd been staring off into space, and I wasn't sure if he had heard me. "I said, are you…."

He cut me off. "Do you think there are any girls in Penryn?"

That surprised me. I was thirteen, and so girls were definitely on my radar, but not really as anything more than abstractions. "Probably. I guess they've got girls in the country, too. How come?"

Scott kicked a rock absentmindedly. "Probably not as many as in Sacramento, though, huh?"

I pondered that for a minute. "Nah, probably not."

"And they probably aren't as pretty, huh?"

"I don't know, but Dwayne said there is a good looking one named Valerie Smith that is foxier than any girl in the state."

Scott paused and tightened his lips. "Huh, interesting."

I kicked a little bit of dirt under my right shoe and then shrugged. "How come?"

Scott glanced furtively around, but the other three were busy with the chipmunk hunting. "It's just…don't say anything, okay?"

"Sure."

"Especially to Mom and Dad," he warned.

I nodded. Our folks had a strict rule about not dating until we were sixteen, so this had to be juicy. Scott sighed. "Me and Chrissy Thompson kissed last night."

I gasped. Chrissy Thompson was one of the cutest girls in our Sacramento neighborhood. Scott was a good brother and all, but I never saw him as the type of guy who could get a girl like her. "How? Where? What were you…."

Scott cut me off. "It doesn't matter. The point is, she and I finally kissed, and now we're moving up to this place in a couple weeks, so it doesn't matter anyway."

I was at a loss. What kind of advice was I supposed to give my older brother about girls? I had just realized the year before that they don't have cooties as we used to believe when we were younger. Now it made sense why Scott hadn't seemed as happy about moving up here as the rest of us. I was just about to try to put something together to say when a sparkling light-blue Honda mini-bike swerved off the dirt road and crashed through the open field toward us. We instinctively cringed as the bike came up to us, but it stopped well short and covered us with dirt clods. The driver proudly dropped his kickstand and walked towards us, swaggering like he was Evil Knievel.

"Hiya, Dwayne," he said. "Whatcha got here?"

"Hey, Stewart," Dwayne responded, walking up next to us with David and Floyd in tow. "These are the new guys I was telling you about last week."

We were staring, and not just because of the bike. Stewart was pretty normal looking at first—dark tousled hair, stocky build, and red and blue plaid shirt—until I noticed his pants. He wore a pair of faded blue jeans with an extra pair of back pockets sewn into each side of his legs. These weren't jeans pockets either. The one on his right was made of tan corduroy, and the one on the left looked like it came from a checkered leisure suit like the one Henry Shack wore at his car dealership in Sacramento. Those extra pockets were full of who-knew-what, weighing them down and making them hang just below his waist. *Is this a Penryn fashion statement or is he just too poor to buy new pants?* I wondered.

"Hey," Stewart offered with a grin. When he smiled, he got even weirder. His dirt-encrusted face contrasted sharply with two huge, white front teeth that made him look just like Bugs Bunny. Scott diplomatically tried to overlook them, but David and Floyd were giggling behind us. Stewart noticed.

"What's so funny?" he asked suspiciously.

"What happened to your teeth?" Floyd asked with a high-pitched giggle. That earned him a swat from Scott, which only made him and David laugh harder.

"What about 'em?" Stewart demanded.

"Are they real? Did you get em' with your Halloween costume?" David tittered.

Stewart just stared at them and then lowered his gaze. They kept giggling, but eventually they realized that he wasn't laughing. Stewart's grin was gone, and his expression showed anything but appreciation for their joke. "These, tubby," he pronounced with an angry glare at David, "are my real teeth. You wanna make something out of it or what?"

David paled. Normally calling him "tubby" would be a mortal insult, but despite his ridiculous pants and buck teeth, Stewart didn't look like someone he wanted to mess with. He was much shorter than all of us except Dwayne, but his very wide stocky build made him look more impressive. His cool mini bike, bulky size and general grunginess caused David to be warier than he normally would.

The tension was broken by a low chuckle. We realized it was coming from Dwayne. Gradually, Stewart loosened up and smiled again.

"What's so funny?" I asked, perplexed by the change in Stewart's demeanor.

"Aw, he's just yankin' your chain," Dwayne replied. "We all call him "Tooth" around here."

Stewart stepped up and slapped David on the back. "That's Tooth Toothly to you, Tubbs."

"We call him "Stoopy," Floyd offered.

"Stoopy," Tooth echoed, looking appraisingly at David. "That figures."

Dwayne introduced the rest of us, and Stewart decided to join up with our expedition. "Where ya headed?" he asked Dwayne, who had taken the unofficial role of tour guide.

"We were headed down the road as far as the Dark's place," Dwayne replied.

Tooth scoffed. "Dark's? Nothing worth seeing there."

"Who are the Darks?" Scott asked.

"Bunch of hippies who live down that way," Stewart answered, jerking his thumb behind him. "It's more of a compound than a home, and you never really see any of 'em around."

"They've got kids, though," Dwayne insisted, "and there's always something kinda weird going on around there."

"You wanna check that out on your time, go ahead. I'm guessing these city boys have seen hippies before, ain't that right?"

We all slowly nodded. Actually, I was pretty curious about the Darks, and we hadn't really seen much of hippies in our neighborhood in Sacramento. Still, when you're from the city, you don't really want to admit that you haven't seen something that a country boy thinks you should have seen. So, we put the Darks aside for now.

We were walking as we talked. Stewart walked his Honda beside us. He and Dwayne were discussing a boy named Owen. "He should meet these guys," Tooth said. Dwayne agreed, and so we started heading towards Owen's house which, we were told, was back past our house and on the other side of a hill. On the way we walked by our new partially-built house, which looked like it was almost finished. The freshly laid grey stucco was on and some men were there taking down the scaffolding. I mentioned to Stewart that this was our new place. He looked suitably impressed, then asked, "They told you about the ghosts, right?"

My brothers and I stopped dead. "Ghosts?" Floyd stammered. It was bright daylight, but we all felt a shiver of apprehension.

Stewart and Dwayne looked solemnly at each other. "They don't know about the ghosts, do they?" Dwayne sighed.

Stewart took it upon himself to point out the ridge just east of our house. "You've heard the trains running through Penryn, right? Behind those tracks on the other side of that ridge is Bickford Ranch, and that's where your ghosts live."

"Why are they there?" Scott asked. He was the oldest, so of course he seemed a bit skeptical.

Dwayne took up the narrative. "There are dozens of abandoned gold mines out there, and miners used to die in accidents all the time. Plus, no one goes there anymore, so criminals from the cities dump dead bodies there a lot."

"*Criminals from the cities?*" I mimicked, falling in with Scott. "You telling me Hoffa's buried there?"

Tooth shrugged. "Make fun of it if you want, city boy, but Dwayne's telling the truth. Those tunnels stretch for miles underground, and they're full of water, critters, and anything you can imagine. A couple of guys from school went up there last year and came back crying. They still won't talk about what they saw there."

After reaching the top of the small hill where our house sat, we began to traverse down the other side, pushing away the occasional small willow tree growing among the tall grass. We were getting close to the western end of our ranch now. In the next field, cattle roamed freely. The field was encircled with an old barbed wire fence. An old beige single-wide trailer sat on the crest of the hill some 100 yards from our position. I started to slip between two of the wires when Dwayne grabbed me. "Don't go in there!" he hissed.

"Why?" I asked. "Is this place haunted too?" Scott sniggered, but David and Floyd were wide-eyed.

Dwayne shook his head. "That's Old Man Shepman's place. No one goes in there."

Stewart nodded in affirmation. "You see that

trailer, city boy? Old Man Shepman sits on his rocking chair up there all day long, just waiting for kids like us to come across his field and spook his cattle. He's got a shotgun on his lap, and as soon as he sees you, he'll fill you full of buckshot. He's got no wife, no kids, nothing but a grudge against kids trying to cross his property. Some of the guys at school…."

"Lemme guess, they crossed the field last year and came back crying?" I guessed.

Stewart's face darkened. "Cross it, then," he said, pushing me towards the fence. "Don't say I didn't warn you."

Scott stepped towards me. "This probably isn't a good idea, Fred," he said softly.

I shook my head. "What, you believe in the ghost stories, too?"

"No, but I do believe in farmers with shotguns. C'mon, let's just go around."

"No way. Go around with the rest of them if you want, but I'm going across."

Okay, so David wasn't the only stupid or stubborn one in the family. Still, I was tired of being taunted by Stewart and his stupid stories, so I was crossing the field even if hippie ghosts came out blasting with shotguns.

Dwayne grabbed me before I went in. "Look, if you're gonna do this, you see that creek over there?" It looked to be about the length of a football field from the fence line. "Make it across that, and Old Man Shepman's bulls won't chase you anymore. He might still shoot you, but at least you'll be safe from the bulls. We'll meet you over there."

"Thanks," I nodded, and then slipped quickly between the wires.

Everything was quiet as I slowly walked through the field. In fact, it seemed too quiet. The creek bed seemed miles away. About halfway between the fence and the creek, two huge black bulls grazed. They were surrounded by several cows and a bunch of little calves. I was trying to be quiet, but they heard me and looked up. The mothers didn't take much notice of me and went back to licking their young, but the bulls were another matter. They stared as if I was coming to butcher their families and sell them as hamburger meat. I angled as far to the right of the bulls as I could and tried to think vegetarian thoughts, hoping that I could somehow transmit to the bulls that eating them was the last thing on my mind.

Old Man Shepman's trailer was up the hill to the left. I only dared to look up once, but didn't see any signs of activity. My heart rate slowed a little bit. *Sure, Stewart, waiting all day to shoot kids,* I thought. *Maybe he's busy playing poker with the ghosts at the mine, or maybe he and the Darks went down to LA for a rock concert.*

Despite my attempts to angle away from the cows, I was getting really close. Now the mothers were starting to pay attention to me. My path took me right next to one cow who was nursing two young calves. She looked up and bellowed at me, and I heard a rumbling snort from the bulls in reply. My guts were screaming at me to run, but I knew that sudden movements would be more likely to lead to a stampede. *Easy, Freddie,* I told myself, inching cautiously away from the cows. The bulls followed my every move. I risked a glance at the creek on the far side. Five boys were standing there. I could see Stewart's buck-toothed smile, and I imagined him laughing at me if I ran away. I steeled myself up and began to walk casually.

My feigned confidence must have relaxed the bulls, because I made it past them and the herd with no problems. With about fifty feet to go I started swaggering. My brothers saw and burst into relieved smiles. Then Floyd did something incredibly, incredibly stupid. "Good job, Freddie!"

he screamed in his high voice.

If my walk had relaxed the cattle, Floyd's scream infuriated them. I heard an angry bellow behind me, and looked instinctively at the bulls. They weren't moving, and then I saw a blur behind them: The mother cow who had eyed me earlier was charging full tilt. I froze for just a second, and then I ran as fast as I could for the creek. I had a pretty good head start, but she was a whole lot faster than I. *Let me be Fast Freddie today,* I prayed as I ran.

The creek was right in front of me. A half-rotted pine log lay across it, connecting both banks. I risked a glance behind me as I approached the creek, and the cow seemed to be right on my tail. Every muscle in my body tensed as I flew towards the creek. With about five feet to go, I heard a snort right at my ear and leaped as far as I could. By some miracle I landed right on the log and kept my balance. Running like an Olympic gymnast, I chugged across the pine and collapsed on the other side of the bank.

Dwayne had been right. I looked back from the ground and saw the cow pawing furiously at the water, but it made no move to chase me any farther. Her young ran up behind her, and she turned away from me with one last angry snort and went back to licking her young.

The others gathered around me. "You okay?" Scott asked breathlessly.

I nodded, mindful of Stewart's smirk. "No big deal," I said as nonchalantly as I could, then I turned and swatted Floyd. "Don't yell like that next time! What's the matter with you?"

Floyd's lip quivered, and his eyes filled with tears. I felt bad instantly and apologized. Stewart gave me a slap on the back. "Nice job, city boy. I didn't think you had it in you."

I glared at him. "Where were the gunshots?" I demanded.

Stewart laughed. "Guess you got lucky this time. C'mon, let's go meet Owen."

Owen Hawk was one of five children. His dad had died when he was very little, and his mother had a tough time raising the children by herself. When we reached his place, he was at the door of their barn beating a rug. Owen was tall and skinny, and had long, curly blonde hair. "Can you leave now?" Stewart asked.

Owen nodded happily. "My brothers told me about something worth seeing. Follow me."

He led us across his yard to a small grove of trees. Quickly he motioned for us to be quiet by putting his finger over his lips, and then he dropped into a crouch and started frog-walking into the trees. My brothers and I had just met this kid, and we started snickering, but Dwayne urged us to be quiet. Scott rolled his eyes at me, but we decided to indulge the country boys one more time.

Our indulgence was well worth the effort. The trees ended at the top of a small hill, and Owen pointed to the bottom. I heard the faint sounds of splashing and female voices below. Carefully, we stuck our heads out and looked.

A small country house sat in the middle of the clearing with an old doughboy swimming pool in the backyard. Most of the details of the house flew right by us as we focused in on the main event: two attractive blonde girls swimming in the pool. They were pretty far away, but we could see enough to be sufficiently impressed. "Those are the Deerdra girls," Owen whispered. "Sometimes they go skinny dipping."

They were wearing white swimsuits today, so apparently today wasn't our lucky day. Still, it was a sight worth seeing. We watched for a while, and then Owen broke the spell. "We best be getting back," he said, pointing to a dust cloud coming down the road. "Their pa doesn't take kindly to trespassers."

Scott was particularly absorbed, and Dwayne and I practically had to drag him away. "No girls in Penryn, huh?" I whispered to him. He smiled, and apparently Chrissy Thompson didn't seem to matter as much anymore.

As we turned to creep away, David tripped over a branch. He fell with a loud grunt. "Who's there?" one of the girls yelled. We froze for what seemed like eternity. Then the other girl spoke up.

"Hey boys," she said in a voice that sounded like what I was used to hearing on TV. "Wanna come skinny dip with us?"

That was it for Owen. He bolted, and the rest of us followed hot on his heels. I was more afraid of them and their pa than I was of the mother cow. Scott, I noticed, was running with a smile on his face.

Chapter Four
Bear

I stretched out in my new bed with a sigh of contentment. Our house was finally ready, and I loved my new room. Floyd and David were miffed that Scott and I each had our own rooms and they still had to share. "Tough," Dad had finally barked when David complained for the fourth time. "Keep whining about it and Floyd gets his own room too. You can sleep out in the shed." That shut David up pretty quickly.

David definitely was missing out, though. My room had a great view of the Sacramento Valley, and that morning I had been able to see the snow-capped top of Mount Diablo. My window was open, and the fresh air smelled clean, crisp and refreshing. There was no usual smog that we would smell on occasions in Sacramento. I could never leave my window open in Sacramento because Mom was afraid a burglar would get in. Our new house sat at the end of a dirt road surrounded by large open rolling fields that protected us from people. For the first time in some years we did not have to worry if we kept all of the windows open both upstairs and downstairs. In fact I was sure Mom and Dad didn't even lock the doors at our new place.

My new bed was a real change from my old single bed that had been rapidly becoming too small for my growing body. My new bed was actually not new but a used queen size bed from Grandma Davis. Unfortunately, Grandma decided to tell me the history of the old bed. She told me that the bed was used by Great Grandma Ward for many years and that she actually died in it just a few years ago. So, instead of getting rid of the old bed, they decided to give it to me and not tell me about the history of it until the day I moved into our new house in Penryn. Though I felt a little uneasy and a little creepy, I fell asleep that first night dreaming of adventures with my new country friends. *If this isn't heaven,* I thought as I drifted off, *it's awfully close.*

Normally, Dad had to bang on the door to wake me up before eight. Early this morning, however, a bird calling from under my window woke me up.

Excitedly, I jumped up and ran to the window to see my new friend. After rubbing my eyes a few times, I gazed out the window to see two beautiful pheasants perched in our newly planted lawn, enjoying the seed that Dad had laid down the day before. I had read a book on bird watching a couple months ago and enjoyed recognizing the male by the colorful feathers and red ring around his neck. "Scott!" I yelled. "Open your window!"

I heard a groan and then within a few seconds I saw his window in the room next to mine opening. The screens had not yet been put on so I saw Scott as he stuck his sleepy-hair head out of the window. "What is that?" he muttered, sleepily rubbing his eyes.

I pointed down to the lawn, and Scott saw the pheasants. His reaction was a bit different than mine. "Dad's not gonna like that."

Downstairs the front door flew open with a crash. The pheasants quickly scattered as Dad, wearing only white Fruit of the Loom underwear, angrily ran into the yard, stomping and swearing at them to get off his lawn. Scott and I shut our windows, chuckling. We didn't like it when Dad was angry at us, but his wrath could be pretty funny if it was directed elsewhere.

The other two boys were up pretty early today as well, but not because of the pheasants. Mom and Dad had promised us that we could have a dog when we moved to Penryn, and today was the day that they were going to make good on their promise. After a typical Mom Nickel breakfast of pancakes, eggs, and bacon, we clambered into the car, arguing about what we were going to name the new dog. "I want to name him 'Lassie,'" Floyd announced as he buckled in.

"That's a stupid name," David mocked. "Let's call him 'Thunder.'"

"Why? Are you naming him after one of your farts?" I teased.

"Shut up, stupid!"

"Wow, another original one. Keep 'em coming Stoopy."

"Let's wait 'til we see it," Scott intervened. Naturally, that wasn't enough to keep David and me from arguing, and we were still going at it by the time we reached the Belson's home. Sandy, their German shepherd, had just had a litter of puppies. We had been excited about a new German shepherd, but Mom had explained that Sandy had "gotten out on the town" and had had a litter of mutts instead of purebreds. That didn't matter much to us. David and I finally abandoned our argument as Dad drove past the Belsons' white picket fence. When Dad pulled up to the top of the steep dirt driveway, all four of us were out of the car before Dad had finished braking. "Boys, get back here!" Mom called, but it was too late. It was usually too late by the time Mom called at us to get back, but she still kept trying.

As usual, I was the fastest. Mom told us before we arrived that Sandy had the puppies in the garage and that with Mrs. Belson's permission we could go look. I saw a door open on the side of the garage, and so I made my way up a set of stairs in lickity split time. Scott, however, was hard on my heels with Floyd and David way behind. As I turned the corner into the dimly lit garage, I learned my first lesson about country dogs: they are not like tame leashed city dogs. We were used to Grandma Davis' old poodle Pixie, who acted like she was ninety-three and could hardly squat to go to the bathroom.

Sandy, however, could definitely use her legs. As soon as I took a few steps into the open garage door she was up growling, standing protectively between her puppies and me. I braked quickly. "Good dog," I muttered in what I thought was a soothing voice.

I took a tentative step backward, and Sandy snarled and leapt toward me. Quickly I turned and ran back the way I came. Scott was just reaching the top of the stairs when he saw me springing down them, the snarling German Shepherd hot on my heels. "Look out!" I yelled, bowling him over as I fled. Scott fell to the side, but Sandy ignored him as she continued to chase me down. *This seems awfully familiar,* a part of my brain thought as I recalled the cow episode from last weekend.

The station wagon and my family were in front of me, but there was no way I was going to reach them in time. Just when I thought Sandy was about to get me for good, a loud voice yelled "Heel!" from the front door. The snarling and barking behind me did not stop though. In a panic I could see that the closest back window of the station wagon was open and no one was in the car. Feeling the hot breath of Sandy on my heels, I leapt in the air like Superman, putting my arms out in a streamline fashion, hurling my body through the open window and onto the vinyl, green back seat bench. Relieved, I lay there catching my breath looking back to see Sandy scratching and clawing at the top of the door, attempting to reach me.

Within seconds a hand grabbed her black collar and pulled her back.

I leaned up a little bit only to see a strange man holding Sandy and my dad's huge shadow looming over me. For a second I was afraid he would be mad at me, but then I heard him chuckling. "Let that be a lesson to you, Freddie," he said, opening up the door. "Don't mess with a country mother dog and her pups, even if they are three months old."

"Yes, sir," I said meekly. Dad chuckled again and took me over to meet Mike Belson, the owner who had just saved me from certain death. "Thanks, Mr. Belson," I said.

"No problem," he said, laughing. Mr. Belson was an older gentleman who looked the part of a lifetime Penryn citizen. "You're pretty fast, son. Sandy normally catches the boys she chases. Practically chewed the leg right off one last week." He and my dad shared a laugh at that. I wasn't sure if he was teasing or not. I hoped he was.

Mr. Belson hooked Sandy up to the tree and then took us all into the garage, making sure to stay between Sandy and us. She was pretty docile once she was chained to the tree and could not see us fondling her puppies. All of the puppies were cute, but it didn't take us long to decide on one particular pup that looked just like a little bear cub. She licked Scott's face when he picked her up, and the bond was immediately forged. She was all black with brown markings on her chest, nose, and part of her under belly. "Can we have this one, Dad?" Floyd asked, gently putting her back with the other puppies.

Dad looked over at Mr. Belson, who shrugged. "Fine with me, Hank," he said. "Always thought that was the ugliest one anyway, so you're welcome to her if you want." Floyd looked at Scott, David and me and we all nodded our heads in approval.

That pup didn't have a moment to herself for the rest of the day. Despite our earlier argument in the car, we had no problem forming a consensus on her name. Soon Bear, as she came to be known, followed us everywhere we went.

The next day was one of the most exciting days of my life. I couldn't wait to get out and explore more territory with my new best friend Bear. At the crack of dawn I was bounding down stairs to see if Bear was okay. Mom put her in the downstairs bathroom in a large box with a ticking clock inside to make her feel like she was near her mother. I guess the sound makes the puppies feel like they are hearing their mother's heart beat. To my surprise, I was not the first person to arrive, but, in fact, was the last boy to greet Bear for the day. I had to patiently wait for my turn to hold and caress Bear.

Over the next two months Bear grew fast, and it was becoming evident that Bear was half German shepherd and half Black Lab. She was going to be a big dog and was already forty pounds at only five months old. Everywhere we went Bear would follow, making sure that every place we went and everything we touched was smelled. In just those two short months she had learned to sit, lie down, fetch something when commanded, and shake hands on command. This dog had, in just a couple of months, become all four boys' best friend and companion.

"Watch this Fred," Scott said as he pulled a piece of ham out of his pocket.

"Look what Bear has learned." Scott took the small piece of ham over to Bear who by this time was sitting attentively, watching Scott's every move.

"Stay, stay, no, no," Scott continued to say to Bear over and over as he lay the piece of ham on the top of her long light brown and black nose. Bear stood there as stiff as a board, her left rear leg shaking feverously.

Scott turned to me while still holding out his right arm and index finger at Bear. "You see, she minds everything I say." Bear still sat there looking at the juicy ham on the top of her nose.

"Ok, go ahead," Scott exclaimed in an excited voice. Bear then shook her nose causing the ham to fall near her mouth. Within a split second the ham was in her mouth and gone.

"Now that's a trained dog," I said while nodding my head toward her.

Bear was fiercely protective of our property and of us boys, even at her young age. Any visitor that arrived was greeted by Bear who would bark ferociously. You could tell when she was truly upset because the hair on the back of her shoulders would stand up. Funny, though very aggressive and mean to strangers, she would never bite anyone. She was what every country boy had dreamed of as a pet. Dad had planted oats in the big front pasture near the creek at the same time as the front and back yard lawns were planted. After only a couple of months the oats were at least two feet high. This soon became one of Bear's favorite play areas. Almost every day we would see her bouncing and bopping around the high oats, looking for pheasants, quail, rabbits or any other type of animal or bird.

Chapter Five
Dinner at the Toothly's

Tooth's voice rang through our pasture as he walked towards me. "Whatcha doing, Freddie?" he yelled.

"Quiet!" I hissed, waving him down. "You're worse than she is." Bear had started barking like crazy again, and the sound of wings flapping from the top of the birch tree told me that today's mission would go unfulfilled. I looked up with a sigh to see the finches flying out of my BB gun's range.

"Sorry about that," Stewart apologized as he came closer. He reached down to pet Bear, which I thought was mighty kind of him considering she had ruined each of my hunting attempts that day. A couple of quiet bursts sounded from the other side of the pasture, accompanied by more finches flying away. We heard a quiet curse as Scott dropped his gun in frustration.

"His aim still ain't any better, huh?" Stewart asked.

"Nah, but at least this stupid dog doesn't follow him around while he's trying." Bear had given up barking at the birds and decided to latch on to my leg. I couldn't stay mad at her for long, so I wrestled with her as Scott came over, and he and Stewart chatted a bit.

"Hey," Tooth asked. "You two wanna come over for dinner tonight?"

Scott and I looked at each other and shrugged. We had met Stewart's parents a few days earlier, and they seemed nice enough. "Sure, I'm hungry," Scott answered.

"Great. Go tell your mom so we can go."

"Nah," Scott said. "We can call her from your place. Plus, it doesn't get dark until about nine o'clock and mom only cares if we haven't checked in by dark."

The Toothly house was on top of a hill a mile or so away from our place. Stewart's parents were interesting people. Their names were Bob and Maureen, but we called them Brother and Sister Toothly since they went to our church. Sister Toothly was a lot like our other friends' moms both in Sacramento and here in Penryn: a short, plump, happy little lady who always sang cheerfully to herself while she cleaned, cooked, and did the laundry. In the short time that I had known her, I had never seen her mad, say any words in anger, or ever frown.

Brother Toothly, on the other hand, was definitely different than any dad we had encountered, *especially* ours. While Dad was a huge guy, Brother Toothly was tiny and might have weighed as much as his wife if he were wearing wet clothes. Also, unlike my dad, he smiled all the time... and whistled, of course. He had been building a huge rabbit cage when we were over earlier, and just whistled old church hymns over and over while he hammered. "He loves those rabbits," Stewart had confided, and he certainly looked like it as he tenderly placed each one in its own individual little cell.

"Can we hold one Stewart?" I asked in a whispered tone.

"No way," he muttered. "My dad does not let anyone touch his prized rabbits."

I tried to imagine my dad hugging a bunny, and the image made me laugh under my breath for a number of minutes. I could see Dad throwing one of those rabbits in the air as far as he could. Brother Toothly, though, clearly had a love and reverence for the little creatures.

We hadn't explored much of Stewart's property yet, and he was quite happy to show us around. One of the first things we came across was a small algae-covered pond. Stewart motioned for us to be quiet when we got close to it, and then he hunkered down to creep close to the shore. "You got girls swimming in here?" Scott asked, and we all chuckled, remembering the Deerdra girls. The last few times that we went over to Owen's house, I had seen Scott slyly making his way to Owen's grove a couple of times for a little more "reconnaissance work," as he called it, but I usually pretended not to see it.

"No, but maybe these will turn into Deerdra girls if ya kiss 'em," Stewart answered, motioning us down. We were intrigued, and crept forward after him. "Grab some rocks," he hissed over his shoulder, and we quickly did as directed. I dug up three dirty flat rocks that were partially buried only a few feet away from the pond and put them in my pocket.

Scott and I stood upright and peered into the pond. "What are we looking for?" Scott asked after a few seconds.

"Appetizers," came the response. "And get down or they won't come out."

"What won't?" I asked.

"Bullfrogs!" Stewart exclaimed in a frustrated voice.

"I don't see any frogs."

"Of course not," Stewart's exasperated whisper came back. "They're under the moss waiting for your ugly face to go away!"

We crouched down again and waited beside Stewart for about five minutes. My legs started tingling, but every adjustment I made to relieve them was met with a hiss of disapproval from Tooth. Finally, about ten feet to our left, two eyes appeared out from the thin green moss above the water line. Stewart pointed at them with his left hand, motioning with his right for us to stay quiet. I noticed that he had a rock in that hand, but kept quiet. With a blur of motion, he cocked his arm and threw the rock. It came within inches of the frog, who realized that he was under attack and fled below the water. Tooth said quietly, "Fetch." We spent the next few minutes trying to hit the frogs with rocks, but couldn't. Finally after many failed attempts Stewart motioned us over to the west side of the pond behind a large thicket of cattails. He motioned us to crouch again as he cocked and readied his hand to throw another rock. Within seconds a pair of eyes surfaced about four feet in front of us near the shore of the pond. Stewart slowly cocked his arm back as I lay in a semi-elongated position.

As quick as he cocked his hand I heard the sound.

"Pop."

I kept my eyes on the big frog eyes just in time to see the water splash right between the eyes of the frog. The frog instantly disappeared under the water.

"What was that?" Stewart cried as he rose from his crouched position.

I looked over at Stewart and he was still holding the rock in his hand which was now by his side.

"Come and eat boys."

I turned to look behind me to see Stewart's brother, Mike Toothly, a few feet behind me holding a pellet gun in his right hand. He was just in the process of lowering the gun when Stewart piped up.

"That's not fair, Mike."

I immediately turned back around to look at the area where I now realized the frog had been shot and saw an upside down motionless Bull Frog floating on top of the water. The frog was huge; it must have been a good foot long and was extremely fat.

"Stewart! Dinner!" Sister Tooothy's voice sounded from the direction of their house. Stewart sighed, shaking his head back and forth. "No luck for us today, fellas," he said dejectedly. "Of course, I didn't have to cheat and kill one with a pellet gun."

"Guess I'm not the only one with bad aim," Scott teased, giving Stewart a playful punch. Stewart laughed, and they started walking towards Stewart's house. I started to follow, but then remembered something that brought me up short.

"Stewart?"

"Yeah?"

"What did you mean about appetizers?" I asked.

"Frog legs," he answered. "They taste great right before the main course."

Scott and I looked at each other and burst out laughing. "Good one, Tooth," Scott wheezed.

Stewart was smiling, but he didn't seem to get the joke. "Good what?" he asked, puzzled.

pped laughing. "You serious?" I replied.
eat frog legs as an appetizer?"

..., they're really more of a dessert, but seeing as we're having company and Mom already made a pie, she thought these would compliment the meal right nice," Stewart explained.

We were speechless. "Well," Scott managed diplomatically, "too bad we didn't catch any, then." Stewart nodded and kept walking, leaving me and Scott to gape at each other for a moment before we ran to catch up. *Frog legs?* I asked myself again. *Oh well, at least we avoided those.*

"Stewart," I mumbled in an agitated tone.

Stewart turned and I pointed to the pond.

Mike Toothly had a rake and was leaning over as far as he could in attempt to reach the floating frog.

"Oh, don't worry, frog legs take a long time to make. He will throw that one in the freezer for later if it doesn't sink to the bottom of the pond first."

I looked at Scott who clearly had a very worried look on his face.

We were now near the south end of their property, walking through an open field next to the stream that fed the frog pond. We walked up a slight embankment to the road, and then turned off onto the dirt path that led to the Toothlys' house. As we approached their home I smelled meat cooking, and my mouth started watering. "Smells good," Scott agreed, sniffing dramatically for Stewart's benefit.

Our appetites started to plummet, however, when we were met by Brother Toothly sitting on a stump in front of his rabbit cages. He clutched one of his rabbits—the same rabbits that I had seen him hugging and petting a few days earlier—firmly by the ears, chiding over and over again, "Sit still!" The white rabbit was thrashing to try to get away, but the little man's grip was far too strong. He held an axe in his right hand. The handle was old and worn-out, but the blade's edge glistened in the setting sunlight. He noticed us and looked up with a smile. "Hiya boys," he said, panting slightly from the effort of keeping the rabbit down. "Maureen has dinner ready for ya, so go ahead on into the house."

"Okay, Brother Toothly," Scott and I managed to stammer out in unison. I was grateful for any excuse not to watch the execution of the poor rabbit, which still writhed and wriggled in a desperate attempt to escape. Tooth stayed behind to watch the beheading, so Scott and I did our best to walk fast without looking like we were scared at all. I could hear Brother Toothly starting to whistle the church hymns again as in the past. "Why is he whistling?" I whispered to Scott as we hurried closer to the front door.

"Beats me," Scott whispered back. From behind us we heard a loud thunk as the axe struck home. We both winced at the same time and walked up to the door, not daring to look back.

Sister Toothly looked up from the kitchen sink as we gingerly stepped onto the porch and into the open kitchen door. "Good evening, boys," she exclaimed in an excited voice. "Go ahead and wash up and take a seat. We're all ready for you." She gestured towards their small table with a soap-covered hand. It was a small square table that looked great for the four people who usually sat there. Six people, however, was going to be a tight squeeze.

Within a few minutes Brother Toothly came in the house whispering, Stewart smiling at his heels. He washed up and chatted amiably with us as Sister Toothly and Stewart settled in beside us at the table. Scott and I started to relax a bit, although my mind was still churning over the fate of the poor decapitated white furry rabbit. The food still smelled good, though, and the old Corningware dishes were filled with steaming potatoes and what looked to be a fresh salad. I knew that the vegetables would be good because the few times that I had been over to the Toothlys', I had noticed a small but well kept garden with all kinds of vegetables growing on the north side of the house.

Brother Toothly settled into his seat and offered grace. It didn't take long for me to realize that this was going to be a long prayer, one more like a church prayer than a meal prayer. Mom and Grandpa Davis occasionally waxed eloquent in family prayers at night, but never at meal time. Dad would start grunting with hunger after about thirty seconds, so they saved the supplication for the orphans in Vietnam for bedtime prayers.

Stewart's dad, however, was another story. He prayed for every single one of his relatives by name, and by their number. I would have guessed he was related to the whole Kennedy family. He prayed for the President of the United States, the vice president, the leaders of both houses of Congress, and just about every state official and representative that he could remember. The list of requested blessings went on and on: good rain for the farmers, good new teachers for the Penryn schools, an end to the Cold War, the victory of a Republican in the presidential election, Sister Jones' recovery from her fall last week, and happiness and success for all the leaders at our church. I fidgeted anxiously. Sitting still was usually hard enough for me, but sitting during a sermon while hot food sizzled right under my nose was nearly impossible. I peeked at the food with one of my eyes. I could only see the vegetables and the potatoes; everything else was covered with a lid. I wondered why they had a large jar of Miracle Whip on the table. I saw Scott with both eyes wide open and arms folded. I leaned slowly over to him and whispered in his ear,

"Now, that is some nasty stuff." I lifted my chin as if to point to the Miracle Whip.

Scott tightened his lip without looking over at me nodded his head up and down.

Finally, in answer to my own quiet heavenly petition, Brother Toothly said "Amen." Scott and I quickly closed our eyes. We all joined him, and I happily prepared to dig in. "This looks great, Sister Toothly," I said enthusiastically. "I'm hungry enough to eat a horse right now."

"A horse?" Sister Toothly laughed. "Oh, merciful heavens, we couldn't serve horse here!"

"Or frog legs, right, Stewart?" Scott said, laughing back.

We tried not to call each other our nicknames in front of our folks because they would probably discourage it and probably forbid us from teasing each other. Our parents told us that it is demeaning to call someone a nickname that made fun of them in any way.

Brother Toothly frowned. "No luck at the pond today, huh?"

"Sorry, Pops, we didn't but Mike did, but it sunk before he could get to it." Stewart answered.

"Oh well." Brother Toothly heaved a deep sigh. "Those would have gone nice, but the potatoes will have to do." Again I wasn't sure if the Toothlys were serious or not, but I decided to let it pass.

I started in on my potatoes that I smothered with Sister Toothlys' homemade brown gravy, but Sister Toothly interrupted me. "Wait, Freddie, I haven't put out the main course yet." She got up to the counter and came back with a plateful of sandwiches. Stewart murmured happily, grabbing one of the sandwiches off the plate before she had even set it down.

I took mine and examined it. To my chagrin, something that looked like Miracle Whip oozed out of each end of the sandwich. I hate Miracle Whip. The bread was white Wonder Bread, and the meat was brown and had a lot of slimy-looking fat around the edges. It was no meat like I had ever seen before, but it still smelled good. Bracing myself for the Miracle Whip, I opened my mouth to take a bite just as Scott asked what would be a very important question.

"This looks great, Sister Toothly," he complimented her. "What kind of meat is this in the sandwich?"

"Rabbit, my dear," she responded, pouring the brown gravy over her potatoes.

My mouth closed on empty air. "Rabbit?" we repeated with dumbfounded expressions.

Sister Tooothly looked at us as if we were the odd ones. "Yes, dears, rabbit," she repeated, as if we simply hadn't understood her the first time.

Brother Toothly chuckled. "Yes sir, no city cook can fry up a rabbit like Maureen here," he said proudly. His mouth was full, and tiny chunks of rabbit meat flew from his teeth as he talked. "You're gonna have a feast like you've never had before, I guarantee that." The Miracle Whip was now oozing from both edges of Brother Toothly's mouth, the left side more than the right.

No argument here, I thought. *Oh well, maybe if I just ate the potatoes....*

He was still talking, though, holding the tub of gravy in his hand preparing to pour it over his steaming potatoes. "This gravy is also made with rabbit meat," he said as he turned toward me and poured a huge amount of gravy over my potatoes. "There, take some more gravy over your potatoes; it brings out the taste just right."

My stomach dropped and I started to immediately feel sick. Two minutes ago I had been starving, but now eating was the last thing I wanted to do. One horrible thought was nagging at me. "Is this...is this the rabbit you..." I couldn't finish the sentence.

"Chuckles?" Brother Toothly asked, looking shocked. "Of course not!"

I was relieved, but also confused. "So... so you didn't kill this rabbit?" I don't know why that would have made things better, but the idea of eating something that Brother Toothly had personally decapitated really didn't settle well.

"Not today," Sister Toothly said indignantly. "We wouldn't serve guests fresh rabbit. They taste much better if they've simmered for a few hours."

"This here is Boingo and Bonkers," Brother Toothly added helpfully. "They were brother and sister."

Bonkers is right, I thought. My mind whirled as I looked for a way out of this mess. I looked at Scott, who had been very quiet during the whole exchange. He was eating his sandwich at the corners, which allowed him to only eat the bread and Miracle Whip without actually having to chew on the rabbit. I hated Miracle Whip too much for that to be an option for me, but I admired his ingenuity.

"Eat up, boy," Brother Toothly urged, digging into his own plate. Stewart beamed happily as he polished off his first sandwich and dug into a second.

I looked at Sister Toothly, and she smiled at me. I decided to appeal to her. *She's a mother, and she seems way too normal to be part of this rabbit conspiracy.* "Sister Toothly?" I said in a small voice.

"Yes, dear?" she asked concernedly.

"My…my stomach hurts and I don't feel too hungry. Everything looks really good, though." It was lame and I knew it.

She laughed again, an airy laugh that immediately told me that my appeal hadn't worked. "Oh, nonsense, when you came in you said that you were starving! Just have a bite and it will open that stomach right back up."

So much for that strategy. Scott had at least managed to push his food around so it looked like his sandwich was at least halfway eaten. Mine stared at me from my plate, and I could almost picture Boingo and Bonkers looking up at me with pleading eyes from their cages.

Another flash of insight hit me. "Can I use your bathroom?" I asked. "That might do the trick."

"Of course," Brother Toothly said. "Just down the hall." He pointed with his fork, which had a piece of rabbit meat precariously close to dropping.

This next part of the move was the most important. I was holding my sandwich in one hand and my napkin in the other as I stood. As slyly as possible, I did my best Harry Blackstone imperson-ation and passed the sandwich into my napkin, and then cupped the package in my hand and against my wrist. No one seemed to notice, and I silently rejoiced as I headed out of the kitchen and down the hall.

Stewart's voice shattered my brief reprieve. "Why you got your sandwich with you?" he asked.

I was caught, but I still tried to hedge. "I...I'm gonna try eating it as soon as I'm done...you know, it's so good that I want to take it to the bathroom with me to eat." Sister Toothly turned pink when I mentioned the bathroom, and Brother Toothly furrowed his brow at me, but they let it pass. I scampered into the bathroom as quick as I could, locked the door, and then tore the sandwich up into tiny pieces to flush it down the toilet. *So far, so good,* I thought. *I can probably handle the potatoes if I put enough salt and pepper on them, as long as I don't have to eat this sandwich.*

I delayed for a couple of minutes, then flushed the remnants of the rabbit sandwich down the toilet with the exception of a small portion of the sandwich from which I took out the meat and wiped off the Miracle Whip with toilet paper. "Bye, Boingo," I whispered. "Bye, Bonkers."

"Mmmm, that was good," I exclaimed as I stepped toward the table and put the last piece of the sandwich bread in my mouth.

"Feeling better?" Sister Toothly asked when I sat back down. I nodded with as much enthusiasm as I could muster.

"Attaboy," Brother Toothly said, slapping me on the back. "Here, lemme load you up now that your stomach's right again." To my horror, he slapped another rabbit sandwich on my plate, the Miracle Whip oozing out and congealing with my gravy-covered potatoes. Boingo and Bonkers were back, and this time I knew there was no gracious way to escape. Scott looked at me with pity, but I hadn't mastered his food rearranging technique yet, and I was out of options.

Just as I was preparing to take the final plunge, the Toothlys' phone rang. Brother Toothly excused himself and got up to get it, which brought me a moment of relief. Stewart looked at me with concern. "You sure you're feeling okay, Freddie?" He asked between bites of Sandwich number three.

I nodded weakly as the voice on the other side of Brother Toothly's phone became loud...really loud. Scott and I looked up. We knew that yelling. Then we both realized the same thing. "We never called home," Scott muttered. We had meant to, of course, but between the frog attacks and the rabbit execution we had forgotten somehow.

"Your mother doesn't know you're here?" Sister Toothly asked, shocked.

"Your dad's not gonna be happy," Stewart said solemnly. I wanted to ask him if the angry voice on the phone had led him to that brilliant deduction, but I kept my tongue under control. Brother Toothly was apologizing profusely on the phone. He hung up after a while and looked at us with profoundly sad eyes.

"Your pa didn't know you were here, and he said to send you home right away."

My heart leapt with excitement. I was free from the rabbits! Still, Scott and I tried to look appropriately mournful. "Aw, too bad, I was ready for another sandwich as soon as I finished this one." Scott said pointing to his messed up plate.

"Dad's not gonna be fun to live with tonight," I added. We got up from the table. "Thanks, Sister Toothly, Brother Toothly. It was real good."

Brother Toothly looked up hopefully. "You wanna take some rabbit sandwiches with you?" he asked.

We didn't have the heart to refuse him, but the sandwiches ended up buried in a dirt patch on our pasture as Bear even refused to eat the Miracle Whip filled rabbit sandwich. Dad, indeed, was not fun to live with that night, but anything was better than dining on Boingo and Bonkers. I had never been so excited for one of Dad's lectures and spankings in my life. For the first time ever

I did not feel the bamboo hitting my butt; all I could think of was my freedom from the awful rabbit sandwiches.

CHAPTER SIX
THE RIDGE

I ran down the stairs two at a time, driven by the smell of bacon permeating the house. I heard it sizzling on the stove as Mom turned it with one hand while flipping pancakes with the other. The other two burners were covered with pans holding scrambled eggs and hashbrowns. Mom was a great cook, and we could always count on a big breakfast from her before the day started.

"Hi, Mom," I said as I jumped onto one of our three black plastic covered barstools at the kitchen counter.

"Did you sleep well?" she asked with a smile as she deftly plucked some of th sizzling hashbrowns from the pan and placed them on my plate.

"Yeah." After a minute my plate was generously loaded.

"Remember to pray, and no syrup on the first pancake," Mom admonished, shaking a finger at me. I nodded. Mom always said that syrup on the first pancake would make us sick because the syrup was toxic to our system as it would then be the first thing to hit our stomach, but her pancakes were still good enough without it anyway. I closed my eyes and said a quick prayer to myself, then left them closed for a little bit longer so my prayer would look like it was earnest and the appropriate length. Then I dug in.

"First one down again, huh?" Scott asked, playfully swatting the back of my head as he flopped onto the stool next to me. "You're gonna be fatter than Timmy Caldwell (an obese boy from back in Sacramento) before long. Did you get all the hot ones?"

"Don't hit your brother," Mom scolded, shoveling food onto a new plate for Scott. "And there are plenty of hot pancakes for the both of you!"

"Thanks, Mom," he said, making a grab for the syrup bottle. Mom grabbed it too. Scott pretended to struggle for a bit, but then released it. It was a game they played nearly every morning, and Scott still let Mom win.

"So, what do you two have planned for today?" Mom asked as she handed Scott his plate.

"Hanging out with Dwayne and Stewart," I answered with a mouth full of bacon. I grabbed the syrup bottle, relishing pouring it over my second pancake while Scott watched enviously. He hated eating pancakes without syrup. "We're probably gonna go hunt with Bear and our BB guns."

"Don't talk with your mouth full, Freddie," my mother admonished as she cut a few apple slices for herself. Mom cooked big meals, but she rarely ate much of them. "And make sure you stay close; I don't want you getting hunted back by some weirdo like that farmer Shepfield."

"Shepman, Mom," Scott corrected.

"Whatever," she sniffed. "Just don't go anyway near his place."

"Aw, Mom, don't worry about us," I pleaded. I realized that I sounded a little whiny, but sometimes that worked with her. "We've got Bear and the BB guns, so we'll be all right."

"If you think some ragamuffin dog and those little BB guns will save you from a grown man with a shotgun, you've got another think coming," she sighed. You know that guy is rumored as being crazy. He's a war veteran that has gone crazy and lives with no one and talks to no one.

"Yeah, Freddie," Scott sniggered. "Bear didn't protect you from Dad when you broke the lawn sprinkler, did she?"

"Shut up!" I growled, which only made him laugh harder.

After breakfast was over, Scott and I grabbed our BB guns and headed out with Bear at our heels. We were supposed to meet Dwayne and Stewart at the crossroads between the Toothlys' place and Grandma and Grandpa's house. We got there first, and, while we were waiting, I picked up a rock. "Bet you I can hit that tree," I challenged, pointing at a tree about thirty yards away. I was still smarting from Scott's comment during breakfast.

Scott cocked his eyebrow. "Bet you I can shoot that rock after you throw it."

I scoffed. "You're crazy. I bet you a whole extra dinner taco you can't."

"You're on, Nose," he said with a grin. I knew my nose was fine, but that still burned. For some reason Scott started calling me "Nose" a few months before because my nose had grown a little faster than my body and face.

I put my Crossman BB gun on the ground and got ready to throw. Bear immediately began sniffing the gun the minute I put it down.

Scott and I stood on the dirt road where Grandma Davis and Grandpa Davis's road nearly crossed with Stewart's road. I picked up a small rock in my right hand while picking up my BB gun in my left, tilting the barrel toward the ground. Bear was sniffing around my legs, and I shooed her away so she didn't throw off my aim. Scott had his gun cocked and was looking at me smugly. I glared at him, then, with as little warning as I could give, whirled and hurled the rock as hard as I could. The gun popped next to me, but it didn't change the course of the rock at all. I smirked as my rock struck the bottom of the tree's trunk. "Looks like you owe me a taco, bud," I informed Scott.

To my surprise, he was dancing in glee. "No way!" he crowed. "I totally hit that rock! I'm Davy Crockett!"

"No you didn't!" I yelled. "That rock didn't move at all!"

"Of course not, it's too big," Scott said in the authoritative voice that he always used when he was trying to assert his own rightness. "It didn't have the impact to alter the flight trajectory of the projectile, but if you were listening you would have clearly heard the sound of the BB striking the rock as it…"

"Oh, shut up and stop talking like that. It didn't hit and you know it!"

"Wanna bet?" Scott challenged.

"Bet! We just bet on the shot, we're gonna bet again on this? Prove that you hit it!"

"Prove that I didn't!"

Luckily Stewart showed up, which ended the argument that was basically unwinnable anyway. He flashed us his customary toothy smile. His well-used Daisy BB gun was in his right hand, and his pants were even more unusual than the ones that I had grown accustomed to. Today's model was a pair of corduroy bell-bottoms. Instead of sewing front pockets on the front, he had sewn the back pockets of a faded pair of Levis on, one of which had about ten small circular holes. He had also sewn a hammer loop from a pair of painter's pants on his left leg just below the pocket.

Scott forgot about the tacos. "What's with the loop?" he asked.

Tooth looked proud. "Holds the gun so I can carry my kill back home," he boasted, demonstrating. "And," he turned around, showing us his butt, "I've got front pockets in the back since I don't carry anything back there anyway, and these back pockets in my front hold my BBs."

"You're crazy, man," Scott said, shaking his head.

"Say what you want, with your regular Levis, but any idiot can wear those. These pants are the pride of Penryn."

"What're you talking about?" I asked. "No one wears anything like that but you."

"Are you kidding me, city boy? All the real Penryn boys wear these every day to school, and the girls love 'em. You'll see. Some day pants that are different with rips and holes in them will be popular."

Stewart could not convince me because I knew from prior discussions that his parents did not have much money to their name and they struggled to keep clothes on the kids and food on the table. It was probably because his mom was so industrious and frugal that she could not throw away a pair of pants that just had a few holes in them. I'm sure she took a few bad pairs of ripped pants and made one good pair, even though they were different colors.

"Gotta agree with them, Tooth," Dwayne piped up from behind me. We jumped in surprise… again. Dwayne had taken to sneaking up on us the past couple of days, and he was very, very good at it. "My sheep might wear those if they had a mind, but other than that, Valerie Smith is the only person I could see wearing those."

"Who's Valerie Smith?" I asked Dwayne.

"Your new girlfriend," Stewart snapped sourly. He really didn't like being teased about his pants.

"She actually probably will try when she finds out you're the new kid," Dwayne said, thoughtfully. "There are not a lot of new people moving into Penryn, you know. I think the population is up to about six hundred and eighty now.

"Is she cute?" Scott asked. "If so, she's not gonna want anything to do with this ugly character."

"She's a little weird, but she's better than the usual around here," Dwayne answered. "Take Mary Olive, for example. Valerie looks like Farrah Fawcett next to her."

"She really that bad?" I asked.

Stewart pointed at Bear. "Imagine her, but with more facial hair." We cracked up laughing at that one and then Dwayne stopped.

"No, Stewart is just kidding; she is a fox."

Content with dreaming about a Valerie Smith encounter in the future, we headed off for our hunt. Bear came along with us, apparently forgiving Stewart for the insult.

"C'mon," he continued, giving me a little shove. "Let's get out of here."

The three of us fell in behind Stewart. It was a dry summer, and dust clouds followed us as we walked along the old rutted dirt road. Bear wandered back and forth, stopping often to sniff at plants and once to squat to take a dump. Stewart led us down the road and to the left, which took us in a direction that I had never been before. The trees were thicker in this part of Penryn, and they curved over the road and blocked out the sun. A small clearing to the left was the site of a new home going up, and an old drainage pipe to our right spurted out crystal clear spring water. The area became more and more lush with green grass and thick, green, old oak trees around the stream. We were looking for something to shoot, but outside of the construction workers we didn't see any targets. We *were* plenty stupid, but not stupid enough to shoot at construction workers, so we kept going.

"Where're we going, Tooth?" Scott asked.

"Up to the ridge," Stewart answered without looking back.

"The one with the railroad tracks?"

Stewart grunted in affirmation. After a good fifteen minutes we reached a barbed wire fence, and Stewart started to navigate it with practiced ease. He lifted the top wire in his left hand and put his left foot on the second wire, pushing down to make a nice opening. "After you, gents," he said, sweeping his right hand forward in a mock bow.

It was a tight squeeze, but I made it through without stabbing myself on the wire. Scott and Dwayne followed, and then Stewart came through. He smiled triumphantly, but then we heard a loud ripping sound. He looked back in terror to see one of the front pockets from his butt dangling on the fence from a thin thread of fabric. His back was now to us, and we saw his checked boxer shorts through the hole in his pants. It was too much for us, and we started laughing again.

Stewart shook his head. "Mom is gonna kill me," he whispered.

"Hey," Scott said cheerily, clapping him on the back. "I've got an old pair of church pants that don't fit anymore. You want one of those pockets?"

Stewart paused and said, "Huh, maybe this is a new trend? He brightened up considerably, and after a minute he kept leading us towards the ridge. Scott walked up front with him, and Dwayne and I trailed, still sniggering at Stewart's exposed underwear.

It had been almost thirty minutes of hiking before we reached a clearing near the top of the pasture. We had climbed a substantial hill and were very tired. The light golden grass in the top part of the field was just stubble and had obviously been eaten by the cattle. As we approached the top of the clearing, I could hear water running. "Yes!" I loudly exclaimed. I was very thirsty. By now the temperature felt like it was one hundred degrees and the sweat was steadily dripping down my forehead. I don't know why, but we didn't even think of bringing water with us. I turned my head to look around to see where the water was coming from. It appeared to be streaming from a long cement ditch winding around the base of the hill. As I approached just behind the other boys, I looked down at the fresh, cool, fast running water. I knelt down and attempted to reach the water with a cupped right hand, but could not quite reach. I laid my body out flat with my chest hanging over the edge and my legs tucked behind me as I reached to grab a handful of the cool water.

Dwayne yelled, "Hey! Don't drink that or you'll get sick."

I turned to look at Dwayne as I took my first sip of cool refreshing water. "Why?"

Dwayne shrugged. "Dunno, but my dad says you should never drink water out of the irrigation ditch."

"It tastes fine to me!" I exclaimed with water dripping down my chin.

Just then I heard a splash a few feet above me and saw Bear running and playing in the water. The water came up to her neck as she frolicked in the ditch, dog paddling at times to stay afloat. The water didn't seem to be hurting her at all, and I was really thirsty. I continued to drink the water: two, three, four and even five cupped handfulls. It was so refreshing. Still lying on my stomach with legs spread out behind me, I took the water with both hands and splashed it up onto my head and face. Oh, what a relief! I looked to my left and saw Scott in the same position, quickly gulping cupped handfuls of water into his mouth. Bear stopped splashing, and I looked up to see what she was doing. To my horror I saw her standing about ten feet upstream from me in a shallow part of the ditch crouched with her tail up, crapping light brown diarrhea, and around her the crystal clear water was turning slowly light brown. She wasn't the only polluter: About ten feet upstream from her Stewart had his back to us, but it was pretty obvious what he was doing. Stewart had his pants part down dancing and swirling like he was spelling something in the water with his pee.

The realization of what I had been drinking hit me. "Gross!" I shouted as I jumped back, water dripping down my face and onto my shirt. "Whadaya think you're doing?" Happy in his ignorance, Scott was still happily splashing water on his face. "Scott!" I yelled. "Get up, you're drinking pee!" He choked a little bit and came up as well.

Stewart laughed out loud as he pulled up his pants. "Dwayne told you not to drink the water."

Scott slowly arched back from the ditch back onto his knees and picked up his gun off the dirt. "Where now?" he asked, spitting out the remnants of the ditch water. He was angry, but he wasn't going to let it show to Stewart.

"We need to jump the ditch and follow it to the railroad tracks," Stewart explained.

Though it wasn't the widest waterway in the world, the ditch was still a formidable jump for a young man. It looked about six feet wide and four feet deep, and was made of old chipped and discolored concrete that looked like it had been there for many years. There was a two-foot wide strip of evenly compacted grey granite on each side of the ditch: a perfect spot for a long jump landing. The ground sloped down on the other side of the ditch, and I could see large blackberry bushes growing just past the edge. Stewart stepped forward and used his right arm to part through Scott and me.

"I'll go first." Stewart took two steps back from the ditch, rocked forward twice, then paused and walked up to the ditch to again gauge the jump.

"You're going to kill yourself," I advised, folding my arms. Frankly, I would have been okay with that after the last few minutes. Stewart was absorbed in his calculations and didn't hear me as he took five large methodical steps backwards, leaned back, and ran. He planted his left foot on the edge of the ditch and leapt in the air, flying over the ditch and landing on both feet just about six inches past the edge. It was a perfect launch and landing.

Before I could say anything Scott began running. Scott was taller, was wearing new white Converse high tops, and had started his jump from farther away, so this was bound to be a longer jump. He cleared the ditch easily, but landed right at the far edge of the two-foot wide strip of compacted grayish granite next to the hill. A triumphant yell turned into a scream as he tumbled headfirst down the hill, landing right in the blackberry bushes.

"Aaah!" he screamed chillingly. Scott just lay in the berries for a moment then rolled onto his left side with his face scrunched in intense pain. I saw Stewart go to help him up, but I wanted to be there to help my brother. However, it was obvious that any incorrect calculations in my jump would result in disaster.

The ditch looked big under me, and I didn't want to fall in or jump too far, like Scott had. Taking quite a few steps closer to the ditch than Scott had, I ran with all my might, leapt from the edge of the ditch, and landed with one foot on the edge and the other trailing in the water. I knew as soon as that left foot got wet that I was in trouble, and I pummeled face first onto the hard decomposed granite. I saw stars, and lay there for a few seconds assessing my injuries. *Just a few scrapes,* I told myself, trying to make myself believe it. I finally stood up, dusted the tan granite flakes from my face, pants and shirt, and looked up to see Stewart walking around Scott to make sure there were no blackberry stickers stuck to his body.

As I was finishing off my dusting, I heard Dwayne's voice from a few feet away. "Come on guys, you're taking too long," he said impatiently. I looked up the hill. About twenty feet from our position and alongside the same side of the ditch that we were now standing was Dwayne.

I winced, blocking the bright sun on the right side of my face with my open right hand. "How did you get over here?" I asked, wondering how he had been spared my fate. He was little, and couldn't have been a better jumper than I.

"I just walked across that board that is laid across the ditch," Dwayne explained, pointing a little farther down the ditch. Sure enough, a weathered grey, warped 4x6 inch board lay across the ditch. Dwayne looked at the three of us with eyebrows raised and a big smile. "Come on city boys, let's go; remember it's always best to look for an easier way before risking breaking your neck. Anybody need anymore pee to drink or want to jump across any more ditches before we get going?" We stared at him incredulously, and as he turned I heard him mumble, "I should be wearing the Penryn Boy pants."

We walked east along the canal, bending down every few minutes to pick up a rock and throw it in the water. Bear was busily sniffing every other bush and tree and occasionally jumping in and out of the canal. Every time she would come out of the canal she would pause and shake from head to tail getting us wet. Normally, you would avoid such a splattering of water, but with the heat bearing down on us we did not mind.

After another fifteen minutes of hiking, we rounded the bend to the right and saw the irrigation ditch disappear into a large cement opening that was bored into the side of the hill. To our right was a walking path that veered away from the canal. "There are the tracks," Dwayne said. "We're almost there." He walked in the front with Scott closely behind and Stewart lagging a bit after them. I took up the rear, calling Bear every once in awhile to make sure she stayed up with the group. By this time the lightweight BB gun was becoming heavy and I was tired of carrying it. The trail from the irrigation ditch to a seemingly level area was approximately two hundred feet long and straight up. We all had to crabwalk to push ourselves up, and it was hard. I saw Dwayne crest the hill and stop, waiting for the rest of us. *He's small, but he sure is tough,* I thought as I wheezed my way to the summit.

Getting to the top, though, was definitely worth it. "Woohoo!" Stewart crowed. "I'm on the top of the world!" His voice echoed below, and he spun around over and over again until he collapsed in dizziness. Scott and I laughed, still panting, and then we straightened up to look around.

We were on top of the world…or at least on top of the ridge. We could see forever, which to us meant that the smoggy skyline of Sacramento was visible.

"Look," Scott said, pointing. "It's our house." I followed his finger and saw our two-story home. A figure that looked like Mom was walking in the back towards our garden. She looked really far away. "I thought we were on a small hill," Scott continued, "but our place looks like a doll house from here. Good thing Mom doesn't know we're up here."

We continued to walk along the ridge-line, picking up the occasional rock to toss at the railroad tracks or down the hill below the ridge.

"Hey, Scott, have you seen Lynn Smith yet?"

Scott turned back toward Dwayne. "Who?"

"Lynn. She's a real fox. She lives just about a half a mile from your house."

This peaked Scott's interest and intensified his desire to no longer think of his old girlfriend back home.

"Huh," Scott shrugged. "What does she look like?"

Dwayne's eyes squinted as he slowed his step. He raised his arms and hands to the praying position with his hands opened, and bouncing up and down he began to describe the Penryn girl.

"She's tall, has a perfect body, olive skin, long dark hair and piercing light blue eyes." Dwayne tightened his lips and now completely closing his eyes, began to shake his head back and forth. "Yes, humph, nice!" Dwayne was now in another imaginary world.

We were all stopped now, standing and staring at Dwayne. As we stood there, I felt the ground start to shake slightly. I looked to my right and realized that I was standing no more than ten feet from the railroad tracks. The earth continued to move and I heard a dull roar. I had heard trains in the distance before, but this one sounded really close. Black smoke billowed above the oak studded hill, and within a few seconds the front engine of a train rounded the bend about a quarter of a mile away from our position. The front locomotive engine was black and moving at a slow, steady pace toward our position.

"Bear!" Scott shouted urgently. I whirled, looking for Bear. I hadn't really seen her since the ditch. The train was pulling closer, and just then Bear popped up on the other side of the rail-road tracks from an area near the irrigation ditch. Apparently Bear had walked through the large irrigation tunnel that went under the tracks and came up on the other side.

In a panic, we all started yelling with Scott, "Bear! Bear! Bear!" My thoughts raced as I imagined my best friend being hit by the large locomotive.

Bear dashed across the railroad tracks just as the thunderous engines bore down on her. She came running up to me at full speed with only seconds to spare. I dropped my gun to the ground and grabbed her by her collar, hugging her in relief. Scott and Dwayne crowded around her, and over her head I saw Stewart run over to the track and bend over, placing something in the train's path. The engine horn blasted at him: not once, but continuously. Stewart whistled and waved at the train, then started, in a cocky manner, slowly walking back when the front locomotive was no more than ten feet away from him. I held Bear's collar tightly, mak-ing sure that she would not move. Stewart was still slowly walking away from the tracks with a half smile as the train slowly chugged past us, its horn still blaring. The conductor was visible at the front of the train. He looked just like I had imagined a conductor should look, right down to the red beard and mustache. I was excited to see him, and waved with my free hand. He stared us down and responded with a hand gesture that was much different than the excited wave I was giving him. He did not smile, but continued to stare with his arm outstretched and finger wagging back and forth as his engine slowly passed us. The sound of the engines was deafening and Bear squirmed nervously to get away from the noise, but I kept a firm hold on her.

We stood by and looked at all the railcars passing: open cars full of coal, empty flatbeds, some box cars with graffiti on them, and even an occasional oil tanker. It seemed as if the train would never end, and then I saw more black smoke billowing from around the bend. More engines approached, connected in between the two box cars: one, two, three, four more engines all at full capacity, billowing heavy black smoke out of the top of each engine. No one was manning the middle engines as they slowly powered past our position. Just as they passed us, I could faintly hear the front engine horn blow three quick blasts. The railroad cars continued and seemed to never end, but at least the noise died down a bit. Bear finally calmed down, but I still kept a grip on her collar just in case she decided to try running at the train again.

Over the screeching of the railroad cars I heard Stewart grunt. Looking over to my right I saw him throwing rocks as hard as he could at the boxcars. The game was contagious, and our BB guns were forgotten as we joined in. One particularly tempting target soon appeared: a rusty brown graffiti-covered boxcar with an open door. We instinctively changed our aim to try to coax our rocks through the doors and out the other side. As I aimed, I noticed two older men standing on either side of the doors. They were dressed in ragged clothes, and their faces were dirty and beards scruffy. One of their eyes met mine, and I dropped the rock that I had been about to hurl at him. His expression was not the kindest one I had ever seen, and for a second I was afraid that they might jump off the train. Instinctively I reached for my BB gun. The old man's eyes followed my hand down to my gun, which probably looked more menacing from the train than it really was, and he and his partner slipped quickly out of sight. I dropped my gun with a sigh of relief.

"Stop, the caboose is coming!" Scott yelled. Dwayne and Stewart dropped their rocks and stood at attention as the caboose slowly approached. It had a dull, orange color and was clearly not brand new from the factory. We saw a man's arm hanging out the window on our side of the tracks. As the caboose passed, a clean-shaven man with dark black hair looked out at us. He seemed to know what we were up to, and shook his head at us in warning. I glanced around. Scott and Dwayne looked innocent enough, but Stewart was bent down to pick up another rock. This one was about the size of a baseball, and there was no way that the train guard was going to miss seeing that.

"Drop the rock, idiot!" I hissed.

"Why?" Stewart asked perplexedly. I pointed sharply to the train guard, and Stewart sheepishly dropped the rock and waved in apology. "Sorry, didn't see him." We all shook our heads, muttering our ill opinions of Stewart's intelligence, and continued our journey west. Dwayne, who had proved to be a much more adept guide than Stewart, led the way this time. I looked at the view to the left as we walked. Everything looked so small; it was weird looking down at our house and the Toothly house, seeing our parents and siblings walk around the property. They looked like little ants busy doing chores on an anthill. Our parents did not know that we were up on the ridge by the railroad tracks. If Dad found out we would be in for it. Scott and I were warned many times that it is very dangerous up on the ridge by the tracks, and Dad had told us that bums and other strange people roam the ridge area. I also saw what looked like David and Floyd playing in the dirt just below our driveway next to the old plum tree. It was hard to tell exactly as I was too far away to make out faces.

We continued walking along the tracks, picking up an occasional rock and throwing it at something stupid like the side of a hill or the side of a steel railroad track. We had walked about a mile when we rounded the bend where I previously saw the billowing smoke from the passing train. As we rounded the bend, Scott, Dwayne and I suddenly stopped. Stewart kept walking. Up ahead of us was a massive dark tunnel that the train tracks disappeared into. It was huge—about three stories high and seventy-five feet wide—and looked pitch black inside. The top portion of the tunnel was almost completely black from the soot of the years of train smoke. Through the darkness I could see the faint glimmer of the tracks as they curved after about fifty feet. At the very top of the tunnel were about twenty feet of large granite blocks laid end to end. They looked like a mantle on top of a fireplace.

"Hey, Stewart, where are you going?" Scott yelled.

Stewart stopped. He was already standing in the tunnel's mouth. "What's up? Why are you just standing there?" he asked.

"Are we really going through that?" Tooth stopped at that, scratched his nose, and started to walk back towards us with his hands in his front pockets.

"That's not smart, Stewart," Dwayne said quietly. "If a train comes and you are walking along side of it in the tunnel, the force of the air coming off the train will suck you in under the train and you'll die."

"Whatever," Stewart scoffed.

"Fine, go ahead and kill yourself. Not my funeral."

I cleared my throat. "Dwayne, what's on the other side of the tunnel?"

Dwayne's countenance became serious and he looked away. "Bickford Ranch. I've heard that the tunnel is over a mile long and brings you right into it."

"You mean the ranch that has the caves and dead people in it," Scott interjected. Dwayne nodded solemnly. "Anyone live there?"

"Nah, it's been abandoned for years. My dad said there's cows and wild animals there, but that's about it."

"Is there any other way to get there?" I asked.

Dwayne pointed down the steep incline that we had climbed earlier. "Yes, you can go down this hill and walk up Clark Tunnel Road."

"It's a long walk, though," Stewart cut in impatiently, "and we could get there in like ten minutes this way."

"You'd be dead in ten minutes, dummy," Dwayne snapped back.

As they argued, I looked down the hill again. It was steep, and the trail was only about a foot wide. Falling down from this point would be much worse than Scott's earlier fall had been, and I definitely didn't want to hike all the way back and start over.

The argument was still going, and Stewart and Dwayne turned to us. "Your call, city boys," Stewart announced, glaring at Dwayne. "Either we walk through this for ten minutes, which isn't dangerous at all since a train *just* went through, or we go all the way back home and start again."

It was tempting, but we were smarter than Stewart. We shook our heads in unison, and Dwayne smiled gratefully. Stewart was bummed, but he had a consolation plan. "Fine, but you babies at least better be willing to climb up there," he said disgustedly, pointing to the granite blocks above the tunnel mouth.

After he phrased it like that, there was no way we could back down. I was a little worried about another train coming as we climbed, but Stewart was probably right: A train had just come through, so we should be okay. After we agreed, Dwayne reluctantly, Stewart led us to the base of the tunnel. The hill was steep, but it looked manageable. We dropped our guns in the weeds at the base of the hill. Stewart started his climb with the rest of us behind. Bear sat at the base of the hill whining, but she followed us up after a minute.

Stewart wanted to lead, but he definitely wasn't that great of a climber. Every time he slipped he kicked up a big cloud of dust and spewed small pebbles. Scott was directly behind him and got the brunt of it in his face. He cursed quietly after the first few times, and during the short climb I heard Scott swear a word other than "fetch", "flip", "doggonit" for the first time in my life. We made up our own curse words so we did not get in trouble for saying the real thing. The words were always close in sound to the real curse words. Like "flip," "fetch," "futch," "shiite," "damp," and "frekin." I felt like swearing myself: I was getting really thirsty, and even the irrigation ditch water sounded good.

We finally made our way up to the top of the trail. I was the last one to arrive, and as I staggered up I saw Stewart, Scott, and Dwayne standing on top of the large granite blocks that were halfway covered up by protruding dirt and grass. I turned to see Bear wagging her tail right next to me. I was worried that she might fall, but she just barked happily at me. I didn't trust her, so I kept a tight grip on her collar. The others plopped down on the blocks, sitting Indian style, and started throwing small pebbles over the edge.

The view was different here at the top of the tunnel. Three large oak trees halfway up the hill and to our right blocked our view of the Sacramento Valley. To the right next to the old road I saw a beautiful peach and citrus orchard. This was a large orchard, with probably a thousand trees. I looked out from above the tunnel at the tracks that meandered up the slight grade. I wondered what type of work it must have been to blast a hole through this mountain to put in a tunnel.

Tooth interrupted my deep contemplations by getting up and moving closer to the edge. "C'mon," he said, "let your feet hang over the edge." He demonstrated by sitting right on the edge, dangling his feet over the side.

"What?" I exclaimed. "That's too dangerous, man. You could fall and die!"

"You could fall and die!" Stewart mimicked in a high voice. "What's the matter, city boy, is your mommy gonna be upset?" He started making chicken noises at me. Dwayne and Scott sighed and joined him on the edge. The taunting was too much to bear: For some reason, Stewart could get me to do just about anything. I gingerly walked towards them, sat down carefully, and let my feet flop over the edge.

The feeling was surprisingly euphoric and exhilarating. "Well, what do you think? Pretty cool?" Stewart asked approvingly, patting me on the back.

Scott muttered. His face was white and his eyes were wide. "Okay, now we can say that we did it. Should we…."

"No way!" Stewart cut him off. "Spitting contest!" He hocked a big one down, and the boogie hit the rail on the right.

"Nice shot!" Dwayne exclaimed.

"Thanks," Stewart said with false modesty. "Anyone else have that in them?" With that, we began an impromptu spitting contest. None of us, not even Stewart, was able to hit the rail exactly, but it wasn't for lack of trying.

After a while, Bear started whining. She had been happy just a minute ago, and the change confused me. As I stopped spitting and looked back at her, I thought I felt the ground slightly move under me. I furrowed my eyebrow and cocked my head, trying to listen. *That can't be a train, can it?* I thought. *We just had one a minute ago.* The others were still spitting, but the tremors were becoming louder. "Guys," I whispered, "did you feel that?" They ignored me, and I felt it coming again. "Guys!" I yelled. They turned and look at me. "Do you feel that?"

Dwayne was bent over with a long string dangling from his mouth. He turned in surprise, and the spit landed on his knee. "What the…."

Before Dwayne could finish his sentence a loud deafening roar came from the tunnel. The ground shook, causing small pebbles of granite dirt to roll down the hill onto the granite blocks where we were sitting. I looked at my brother and two friends to my left. They had not moved, and the look of fright and confusion on their face probably mirrored mine. I then realized that I was still sitting with the lower part of my legs and feet dangling over the top of the tunnel. For a moment I thought about getting up and running, but then instantly I had a second thought of the possibility of falling off the tunnel while attempting to get up and move. The shaking felt like a small earthquake, and the noise was deafening. Suddenly a blast of black smoke billowed up through our legs and into our face. It engulfed us, blinding us and causing us to cough violently. Finally the smoke cleared, but then another blast hit us. We got a total of four blasts, and when the smoke finally cleared we saw that four engines had passed in front of us. Finally, a string of boxcars followed behind them. The tunnel still shook, but at least the smoke was gone. I rubbed my eyes furiously until my vision was clear again.

Three of us had instinctively backed up as far as we could, but Stewart was still sitting on the edge. He paused for a minute, and then he gargled and spit on one of the boxcars. "Woohoo!" he shouted. "What a rush!"

"Get back here idiot! You're going to kill yourself!" Dwayne exclaimed. Stewart ignored him as he continued to laugh and spit.

Scott and I were both shaking, but then we looked at each other. Dwayne noticed the same thing: All four of us were covered in soot. We looked just like Dick van Dyke did as the chimney sweep in Mary Poppins. It took a minute to sink in, but once it did we started chuckling. Scott started humming the tune of "Chim-Chimeree," and that cracked us up. Stewart looked back and noticed our appearance. He grinned, his huge white teeth shining against his soot-blackened face, and we laughed even harder.

No sooner than we stopped laughing a roar from the tunnel sounded and more black soot and smoke billowed up into Stewart's face. Stewart was the only one still sitting all the way on the edge of the top part of the tunnel with his legs dangling. Stewart put his hands high in the air as the smoke billowed into his face and began to yell "Yaaaaa, whooweeeee." Three engines from the middle of the trains passed, continuing to chug hard to pull the heavy laden train up the grade. Within five minutes the train had passed.

Now standing completely up and as far back from the edge as possible, we turned to Stewart.

"Come on; are you going to sit there forever or come with us?" Dwayne sighed, covered from head to toe with black soot.

"Okay, okay, let's go."

As we started to walk back down the side of the mountain, trying not to fall from the slippery granite trail, Scott and I had the same sobering thought. We stopped and laughed out loud and turned to each other. "Mom's gonna kill us," we intoned in unison. Behind us, Dwayne and Stewart started to sing.

CHAPTER SEVEN
CHURCH

The next Sunday all of us except Dad were in Loomis for church. We walked in single file from the car. Mom and Floyd were a bit behind, and Mom was combing Floyd's hair as they walked.

"Ow!" Floyd complained in his high-pitched voice.

"Stop it, you're embarrassing me," Mom admonished sternly. On Sundays all four of us were dressed so as not to embarrass her: We wore white shirts and ties with dark slacks and dress shoes, and our hair was neatly parted and loaded with enough Bryl Cream to hold it in place against a nuclear blast. Mom still didn't get it that we were dressed funny for Loomis. To find a nice cleaned pressed shirt at church in Penryn or Loomis was very rare. In fact most of the boys white shirts were so old that they were stained a yellowish brown.

We were there early, which was Scott's fault. In our church they give jobs to young men our age, probably in part to keep us coming to church. Boys Scott's age had to prepare the sacrament before the meeting started, so he was there early to do that. Since I was a little younger, I was what our church called a deacon, and my job was to pass the sacrament to the congregation with the other deacons during the meeting.

We entered the double glass doors that led to the foyer of the chapel. The white brick interior and red plain industrial carpet was adequate but not fancy. Pictures of Jesus Christ adorned the clean white brick walls. To our left was a set of dark oak doors that had a small window in each so that people could see in. Scott quickly entered one of those and hurried to the sacrament preparation area up in front of the chapel.

The actual chapel was beautiful. The chapel in Loomis was a bit newer than our old building in Sacramento, and I really liked this one. There were three rows of pews and two aisles, and open skylights streamed the summer sunlight onto them. The walnut oak of the pews matched the organ and grand piano, as well as the sacrament table where the priests sat. That table was off to the right, and it came down enough to cover the feet of those sitting there. Two special pews were in front of them; that's where I sat to do my job.

It was about fifteen minutes before church started, and people were still filing in. This was only our third time coming to this place, so I was still getting to know people. The deacon rows were already pretty full, and I had to squeeze into the second row. Steve was in front, sitting in between Ronny Yelper and a boy named Tony Riser. He turned around to say "Hi." Owen Hawk was next to me in the back row. As the three of us talked, I noticed Stewart get up to talk to the priests sitting at their table in front of where we were sitting. At church Stewart was not allowed to wear what he called his "Penryn Boys" pants with their colorful arrangement of different pants put together. But, to show defiance and at least try to be a little different, he had one denim jean belt loop sewn on his dark blue Angel Flight dress pants.

There were three priests speaking, and they all made an impression on you immediately, especially Willie Butler. He was a huge guy who played defensive tackle for Del Oro High School, and his muscles bulged through his old, wrinkled, yellowish white dress shirt. Jim Grimes looked like a stick next to him, but he was still bigger than us. Next to Jim was Paul Bess, a shorter very stout young man who played football with Willie. Though short and very stocky, Paul had a mean streak in him that we couldn't help but be scared of. All of them were seventeen and were going to be seniors this school year. I was usually too intimidated to do more than stammer a greeting, but it soon became obvious that Stewart was smarting off to the boys, taunting them to the point that they were getting irritated, especially Jim whose eyes were furrowed and lips tight. In fact, it was clear that he was smarting off to them. "Like I'm scared of you," his high voice floated back to us.

Jim looked side to side. "Don't start." Jim's voice was quiet, but scary.

Stewart narrowed his eyes, and he leaned forward, trying pathetically to match Jim's intimidating gaze. "Don't start what?"

Willie Butler leaned over to Jim and muttered something in his ear. The burly young man motioned with his index finger for Stewart to come over closer to the table area. Stewart was brave but at times stupid, and he walked right up and sat down next to Jim. With a big smile, Jim put his right arm around Stewart's shoulders. I thought that Stewart had impressed him with his pluck, but as Jim talked to him I noticed the big muscles in his forearm flexing. Stewart's expression changed from one of defiant curiosity to a cold scared stare. His eyes opened wide and his lips puckered as he looked as if he was about to cry. Willie Butler lifted his head up, looking at the adults in the congregation. No one was paying attention as they all seemed to be talking to one another prior to the start of the services. Jim nodded at Willie. Instantly, and so quickly that I almost missed it, Jim put his hand on Stewart's head and shoved him under the table. I was completely still for a few minutes, but Stewart didn't reappear.

The priests sat straight up with their backs against the pew, benevolent expressions on their faces. Paul Bess looked down under the table and smirked as he shifted in his seat. Jim's expression turned cold as he bent down slightly and shook his head from side to side. Within seconds he looked back up with a wide mischievous smile. I leaned forward and tapped Owen on the right shoulder. Owen turned with a slight grin on his face. "What happened to Stewart?" I whispered, shooting a wary glance at the priests.

"He's under the sacrament table," Owen whispered back.

Duh. "Will they let him out?" I asked, keeping my voice down so the lumbering priests wouldn't hear me.

Owen shrugged. "Who knows? I've heard Jim and Willie tell deacons in the past that they would hold them under the sacrament table if they ever smarted off to them. I guess they have to let him out when church is over, right?"

The service was starting, and Bishop Thompson gently placed his large hands on each side of the pulpit and began to announce the program. I heard what he was saying, but none of it registered as I contemplated Stewart's fate. After a few minutes, it was time for the sacrament. I kept my eye on the priests as Bishop Thompson announced the sacrament hymn and then sat down. The hymn began and the three priests stood up and carefully removed the white sacrament tablecloth. They began to reverently break the bread, but I saw their eyes occasionally glance towards their feet, and a small smile would break through their pious exterior. After the bread was broken and the prayer offered, all the deacons stood up and walked up to the table in an organized line. As I approached the table to receive my tray, I could hear Stewart shuffling around under the table. I cracked a smile and could feel the wrenching in my gut as a laugh was about to surface. *Don't laugh,* I told myself. I managed to keep things under wraps, and was amazed that all of us managed to be reverent even though we knew that Stewart was stuck under the table the whole time. I passed Stewart's parents and, glancing to my left, noticed his mother craning her neck looking for her boy. Her husband was muttering, and I guessed that he thought Stewart had skipped church and was hiding in someone's car listening to the Giants play the Mets. *If they only knew.*

After the sacrament was done, we all walked back to the congregation to sit with our respective families. As I settled into our family's usual pew at the back of the chapel near the double doors, I glanced back at the sacrament table and noticed the three priests still sitting there. This was unusual, as we all usually went and sat with our families after the sacrament was over. They appeared very attentive, especially when they noticed that the congregation was watching them, and they focused very intently on the speaker. "Those boys are so righteous," I heard Sister Bradshaw mutter in front of me. "Look, they are staying reverently at the sacrament table honoring their job." *Right,* I thought skeptically.

The back door banged open and shut with a crash, and I noticed Stewart's dad storming outside. He was probably going outside to look for Stewart, and if he were anything like my dad he would tear every car apart looking for him. I wondered what he would do to the priests if he figured out what was going on.

"Is Stewart sick?" Mom asked in a concerned tone. "I didn't see him passing the sacrament today." That was almost enough to make me start laughing, but I kept it under control. Instead, I just shrugged and kept looking at the speaker, whose droning seemed to have lasted forever. As the service dragged on I noticed Stewart's mother and brother quietly slip out. The priests cracked a smile at that, but quickly resumed their attentive expressions.

When the service finally ended, the congregation began to disperse to their different Sunday School classes. I lingered behind for a little bit. The priests stayed at their bench until just about everyone had left. Jim leaned under the table while the other two looked to make sure that no adults were paying attention. Willie tapped Scott, who whispered something sharply. Then Stewart's head popped up from the table. His hair was mussed, and he looked like he had just woken up. Jim pulled him the rest of the way up and pushed him into the aisle, and the three priests walked out the side door exchanging high fives. Stewart reached in his back pocket, pulled out a comb, and began to comb his hair as he walked towards me. "Ready for class?" he asked as he approached me.

He seemed remarkably normal for having undergone such an ordeal. "You okay?" I asked uncertainly.

He shrugged. "I usually sleep during the talks anyway, so it wasn't a big deal." *He's got a point,* I thought as I followed him to our small cinderblock classroom.

There were steel folding chairs lined up against three of the walls. This class was supposed to be for girls and boys my age, but none of the girls had ever showed. Apparently they were all out of town for the summer or just didn't bother coming to church. I grabbed a seat next to Owen, another deacon, Tony, while Stewart huddled up with a guy named Max to share the details of his confinement under the table. Jeff Bost, a kid that I didn't know very well yet, leaned in towards us. "What did you guys do yesterday?" he asked conversationally.

"Nothing much," Stewart replied without even looking at Jeff. His body language suggested that he didn't want to be bothered, but Jeff continued.

"Where did you go?" Stewart ignored him and kept talking to us. Over his shoulder I saw Jeff staring at him, and I felt a little awkward.

"We went to the ridge up by the railroad tracks," I offered. Stewart immediately scowled at me and shook his head, but the damage was done.

Jeff laughed. "Yeah right, you and whose army? Don't you know kids get killed up there?"

Stewart was still scowling at me, so I didn't say anything. Jeff kept going.

"I know you're new here, so I should warn you that those hills near Bickford Ranch are haunted. My mom would kill me if she knew I ever went up there. Have you ever seen any of the caves?"

I just sat there. Max piped in, taking his cue from Jeff. "On the other side of the big tunnel up on the ridge there are a bunch of caves that have dead people buried in them. There's another cave off Clark Tunnel Road at Bickford Ranch that is so big that it has railroad tracks going through it. The cave goes underground for miles, and it's so dark that you can't see your hand in front of your face. There are deep shafts that people fall down and are never found. Some shafts are more than a mile deep...."

I interrupted, shaking my head. "No way."

"You don't believe me?" Jeff asked coolly. When I shrugged, he leaned back against the wall, appraising me. Then he pursed his lips and shrugged back. "Well, if you've got the guts, I'll take you there."

"Yeah right," I scoffed. "Like you've been there."

"Not yet," he admitted. "But my brother Bob has and he told me everything."

"He's right," Stewart agreed, thrusting into the conversation. "I heard the same thing that he did."

"Sure," Owen said sarcastically. "You don't know anything except how to sit under the sacrament table." We all chuckled, except Stewart.

"Shut up," he said with a frown. "They said if I made a noise or told anyone, they would find me later and torture me, but I was quiet because I was tired. Anyway, I know I could have taken them if I wanted to."

"You know," I said thoughtfully, leaning back in my chair, "I bet Jim Grimes, Willie Butler, and Paul Buys have been to Bickford Ranch and the caves."

"Yeah," Stewart replied, "they were probably the ones putting dead bodies in the caves.

"Yeah," Jeff agreed, looking mischievously at Tony. "Dead Deacons."

"Dead deacons, huh," I thought. *"Sounds like an adventure."* My mind began to drift as the teacher started to talk something about the Bible.

CHAPTER EIGHT
SHOTGUN!

The next day, David and Floyd were tagging along with Scott and me, but since we were going to visit Grandma and Grandpa, it was okay with us. Grandma and Grandpa had finished and moved into their new home three weeks after us. The brown and yellow painted home was a quaint rambler with porches on the front and back of the house. The front of the home sat only a few yards from a small duck pond that was fed by a rock filled babbling brook. The area between the home and the pond had recently been seeded for a lawn and had steel fence posts and string strung between the posts to keep out intruders. The construction of a railroad tie set of steps leading from the front porch to the pond had been started with only seven or eight ties temporarily laid in place. We headed right to the usual back porch entrance.

Grandma was cooking breakfast, and the scent of bacon wafted through the open kitchen window as we passed. As we approached, we could see Grandpa through the sliding glass door. He was sitting on their brown suede couch polishing a big shotgun with a rag covered in oil. Grandma was standing over the stove in the kitchen which adjoined the family room, separated only by a white laminated bar with six brown wooden stools. He smiled as he saw us coming and got up to let us in. "Hiya, boys," he said with a smile as he hugged us all in one large group hug. Grandpa's strong arms and large hands engulfed us all.

"Hi," we echoed. Grandma smiled at us from the kitchen, her Clairol died red hair still up in curls. We waved in return, but our eyes were fixated on the huge shotgun that Grandpa had left leaning against the couch.

"What is that, Grandpa?" Scott asked. His tone was almost reverent.

"My new Ithaca shotgun," Grandpa answered proudly, his huge chest puffing out. "Just like my old Winchester I used in Caldwell, Idaho when I was your age."

Our age? I thought excitedly. Grandpa had always told us that he and Uncle Roy had hunted a lot in Idaho, but I guess I didn't realize that they were that close to us in age at that time. *Does that mean that I could shoot….*

"How old were you when you first shot a gun, Grandpa?" David asked, interrupting my train of thought.

Grandpa chuckled. "Probably about your age. Let's see…you're nine, right?"

"Ten," David scowled, folding his arms indignantly. Grandpa chuckled at that, while Grandma clucked at him from the kitchen.

"He knows that, Davy," she called. "He's just teasing you."

"What did you and Uncle Roy hunt, Grandpa?" Scott asked.

"Mostly pheasant and dove," Grandpa answered, easing back onto the couch. The four of us plopped down in front of him. "You see, in our day you didn't just drive down to the supermarket and buy a nicely plucked and wrapped chicken; you had to hunt for your meals and every boy my age had a huntn' dog. My dad's place was about a hundred acres of barley and wheat, so there were lots of good hiding spots for the birds. Same with our neighbors, so as long as we could get the dadgum birds off the land without them noticing what we were doing, we could shoot em."

David blurted out, almost interrupting Grandpa's last word. "What dog?"

Grandpa put his left hand up toward David. "Well just hold your britches son."

"Why would I hold my britches?" David asked

"That's just an old expression."

Grandpa used to always use weird words that we never understood like "you betcha", "yes sirree", "hog wash", "he aint worth two bits", "gonna get a lickin."

"Why, I had two huntin' dogs, Vim and Vigor. They could sniff out a bird that was sitting in a pile of cow manure. I could hunt anywere and find any bird with those bird hounds. When a friend came with me and brought their dog, I told them to just leave them home to save them the embarrassment."

"Did you hunt on any big ranches?" I blurted out. Grandpa furrowed his brow. It was kind of a strange question, so I clarified. "You know, like any special ranches that were up by railroad tracks and maybe had like…you know, mountain lions and dead people and stuff like that?"

Scott was glaring at me, but Grandpa chuckled. "You've been listening to that Toothly boy, haven't you?" I nodded sheepishly. "That's hogwash,

Freddie. Don't you go believing any Penryn tall tales. We had a bucketful of boys like Stewart Toothly in Caldwell, and their stories all ended up being the products of an overactive imagination." The subject was over, at least in Grandpa's mind.

"Grandpa," Scott started tentatively, "can I hold the gun?"

Grandpa winked at him. "Your daddy probably wouldn't want me to do this...."

"Which is a fine reason to do it!" Grandma cut in from the kitchen. All five of us laughed.

"But you really should learn how to handle one of these someday," Grandpa finished. He patted the couch next to him, and Scott jumped up. We all looked with envy as Grandpa held out the weapon on display. "Remember," he cautioned, "this isn't a toy. This is a dangerous weapon and must be treated with respect." With Scott sitting behind him, he pointed out the safety features of the gun so that we could all see. "You should know not to ever point this at anyone, but also make sure it's never loaded in the house. If you're not gonna shoot it, make sure the chamber is open, and before you put it away make sure it's empty. Understand?"

We nodded, and Grandpa relaxed a little bit. "All right Scott, hold out your hands." Scott silently held out his hands, and Grandpa carefully placed the Ithaca's stock in his right hand and chamber in his left. Instinctively, the three of us backed off to the side, and Grandpa chuckled again. "Don't worry, boys, it's not loaded," he reassured us. "Still, you're smart: don't get too close to a gun unless you're the one holding it."

Scott placed the gunstock against his shoulder as Grandpa instructed him, pointing the barrel at the sliding glass door. His right hand found the wooden action on the bottom of the barrel, but just before he pulled it back Grandpa grabbed it firmly. "Not today, son," he said gently.

Scott blinked. It looked like he was snapping out of a daydream, and he had probably been envisioning shooting something...maybe that railroad engineer who had flipped us the bird. "Can I shoot it sometime?" he asked eagerly.

"If your dad will let me, I'll take you hunting next week," Grandpa promised. Scott grinned, and then handed the shotgun carefully back to Grandpa and took a seat on the floor. "Who's next?" he asked, surveying the three of us still sitting and fidgeting on the floor in front of him.

"I am!" I answered, enthusiastically thrusting my hand up as if I was in school. Actually, I never volunteered that enthusiastically in school, but none of my teachers had ever let me handle a firearm in class either. Grandpa patted the place on the couch that Scott had just vacated, and I jumped up next to him. He always looked bigger when I sat right next to him, and I felt tiny as he passed over the shotgun.

"Now, remember what I told you about safety," Grandpa cautioned. I nodded quickly, and my arms shook a little bit as I took the gun from his careful hold. Gleefully, I eyed the shiny barrel, and then took it in the same hold that Scott had and pointed it at the sliding glass door. Beyond it, the red hummingbird feeder on the porch made a great target, and I aimed at it. I then tilted the gun up toward the white and gold sparkly stucco ceiling. In my mind I envisioned the red hair and beard of the railroad engineer, and I smiled as I saw him stare me down menacingly. It was like being in a Western movie. *You or me, pilgrim*, I thought with a tight smile.

"Grandpa," I asked, "you said this isn't loaded, right?"

"That's right."

Then this should be safe, I thought. In my mind the engineer went for the six-shooter at his side, and I gently squeezed the trigger in response. The flash that followed, however, was anything but imaginary. The gun went off with a loud bang, and the butt kicked back hard into my shoulder, knocking me violently back against the couch. Over the roar of the blast I heard the tearing of wood as my shot broke through the ceiling, through the roof and up into the sky. The room seemed filled with smoke, and the acrid smell of powder stung my eyes. I could see the sun peering through the large hole in the ceiling and roof of the house.

I was still clutching the gun in shock. Scott was just staring at me, and David and Floyd had hit the deck as soon as they heard the shot. Grandpa looked shocked for a moment, but turned back to Grandma who had a shocked, disgusted look on her face. "That was smart, Floyd," she proclaimed sarcastically after a brief pause, pouring pancake batter on the hot griddle.

I felt Grandpa's strong hands on the gun, and I relaxed my grip. He had a facial expression that I had never seen on the big man's face: He actually looked scared. With a nod he took the gun from me and walked outside, opening the sliding glass door that had somehow shattered from the sound and stepped carefully around the glass shards on the floor. "You're dead," Scott whispered.

"He said it wasn't loaded," I argued quietly.

Outside, Grandpa stared blankly into space as he opened the chamber. He ejected the empty shell, which I knew was from my shot. Then he cocked the gun again, and another shell came out. This one hadn't been fired yet, and my mouth dropped in amazement. Two more shells came out in rapid succession, and then the gun was finally empty. *There were four cartridges in there!* I realized with a start. "See?" I hissed at Scott. "Not my fault."

Grandpa slowly walked back in the house. "Boys," he said quietly, "your grandpa screwed up today. Remember to be more careful than I was, okay?"

Scott, Floyd, and I nodded quickly. David, who was never known for his sensitivity to awkward situation, piped up right away. "Can I hold the gun now?"

"David!" the three of us yelled at him.

"Oh, for Pete's sake," Grandma grumbled behind us. "Enough of this gun business. The pancakes are done, so who's hungry?"

CHAPTER NINE
WITCHING

The Ollis boys had just moved in with their family on a large piece of property northeast of the Toothly property. It was still August and we all were eagerly preparing for our first trip to our new school in Penryn. Well, we knew it wasn't a "new" school but it would be new to us.

There was a number of Ollis boys: five in all, with two girls as well. Deon was my age and Lane a year older, and their family was one of the last families to move in to our area that summer. Their home and ranch had a much different feel and setting. It was set down in the valley area next to a beautiful stream. The stream and house was surrounded by a number of trees such as pine, oak, willow and aspen. Though dark and gloomy, the setting was beautiful; the rich, brown river bottom soil was perfect for raising crops and a beautiful garden. The wooded area was adjacent to the Toothly's property and strangely the trees ended as the Toothly property began.

I had seen a large Larry Tanko well drilling rig slowly drive down the shared long dirt road. Apparently, though next to a stream, the Ollis family was having problems striking a good well. Both times the Ollises had a well dug, it had come up with less than two gallons per minute and at $1,000 per well, the Ollis family finances were starting to strain.

Now, Father Nickel was someone who grew up in Lake County, CA, where for some reason most men knew how to find deep water. Why and how they knew this I did not know, but I did know that when someone wanted to dig a well, they called my dad and asked him to "witch it." Witching a well took a special talent, and I was soon going to learn the secrets from my dad. When we had gotten our well, the men from the local well drilling company, Larry Tanko Drilling, tried to tell father where to drill for good water. Father ignored them and witched the whole property, and then told them to drill in an area that seemed the most likely to produce a good well. Uneasy with their prospect of hitting water, the Tanko crew reluctantly had begun to drill. Sure enough, after only 120 feet they struck what the workers called an underground river which produced 48 gallons per minute of fresh, clean, cold spring water.

Early one Monday morning in late August, while our family was sitting around the table enjoying a good hearty breakfast, the phone rang. Father answered.

"Hello Vern, how are you this morning?" Father paused and nodded his head up and down as a slight smile formed on his lips.

"Okay, when are they supposed to arrive?" Father paused again, his smile grew slightly.

"Okay Vern, I will see you in an hour." Father hung up the receiver on the wall phone.

"I guess Vern cried "Uncle," Father stated with a smug smile. "He wants me to come over and ditch witch his well before the Tanko well drilling crew arrives." Father leaned back over his plate and picked back up his fork and continued to cut into his pancakes.

Father was clearly taken aback by the call as he had advised Brother Ollis two months ago that he should let him witch his property before they began drilling for water. At that time Brother Ollis politely passed and believed the professional well driller could handle the task of finding a good well just fine.

I followed my father down to the creek near the eastern part of our property. Father was wearing his grey flannel, short sleeved shirt. Father's broad shoulders and large muscle bound arms squeezed tightly against the sleeves of the shirt. Father's First Division Marine tattoo was halfway visible on his right arm and shoulder. He wore his old, dirty, sweat-stained straw cowboy hat and mid-calf cowboy boots. As we approached the creek, Father, without turning to look at me, began to explain the process.

"Remember Freddie, the most important thing about witching a well properly is choosing the right willow stick." I stepped closer to him. Father stepped with his right foot into the shallow part of the creek and began eyeing the various willows growing on the bank. He touched a number of them, bending the small willow trees, looking left and then right at each tree, carefully studying their shape and form. After about five minutes of carefully checking each branch and tree in a five or ten foot radius, Father pulled out a large knife and began cutting at the base of a branch that formed a "Y."

"Back off for a minute son." He gritted his teeth and a few beads of sweat began forming on his nose as he sawed vigorously. Finally cutting through the willow, he stepped back and lifted up the willow branch all covered with leaves.

"Remember, the wetter the tree, the better," Father exclaimed without looking away from the branch. He began to carefully break off each leaf and throw it down onto the ground, all the while carefully eyeing the stick to make sure it was what he wanted. After all the leaves were pulled off he took the stick that now clearly looked like a "Y" and turned it upside down. He grabbed each end of the "Y" with each hand, slowly bending the end of the sticks upward so as to form the shape of a "W" with the longer middle sticking up above the outsides of the "W." The total length of the "Y" stick was probably two feet, the base of the "Y" being a little more than a foot and the "V" part of the "Y" each being less than a foot. I could see the wet green part of the branch protruding through the light grey bark of the willow. "This one will do just fine," he said with a slight grin on his face. Father nodded his head with approval and turned the stick back to right side up and began to walk toward our road. I followed in tow, needing to briefly run to keep up with Father's large, quick steps.

After about fifteen minutes of walking down dusty roads, we arrived at the Ollis home. Dad was a man of few words and said nothing to me as we walked down the road. As we approached the Ollis ranch, the sound of the babbling creek broke the silence, along with the barking of a small black, brown, and white mutt named Klinker. Brother Ollis met us just as we crossed the creek.

"Hello Fred," Brother Ollis said with a wide smile and outstretched arm.

"Hello Vern, how are you?"

Dad was not a member of our church and as such did not want to be called "Brother" by the local church members. Brother Ollis was a former bishop and member of the high counsel, a position of high ranking in the church. He had great respect for my hard working, wise father and as such always addressed him simply as Fred.

In eagerness Brother Ollis started. "We have drilled two wells and have gotten no more than two gallons per minute, clearly not enough to run fresh water into our home." Brother Ollis shifted his weight to his right side and looked sheepishly down at the ground. "The well drillers have charged me an arm and a leg for two dry wells, and I cannot afford to pay them to keep trying. Brother Ollis looked up into Father's eyes. "If I don't hit a good well this time, Fred, I don't know what I am going to do." Father did not say anything, but just kept bobbing his head up and down, lips tight, looking over the back of Brother Ollis's shoulders in attempt to survey the area.

"Where did they tell you the best place for a well is?" Father asked.

"Right over there—you see there are two wells that have been drilled about 100 feet apart." Brother Ollis pointed with his right hand toward two small mounds of dirt that had four inch pvc pipes with caps sticking up about two feet above the ground.

Father said nothing and turned quickly to his right to go around Brother Ollis, and he began walking toward the already dug wells. As he walked, he flipped his stick upside down, grabbing the "V" portion of the stick with the longer part sticking straight up. I walked quickly to catch up to Father, eagerly watching as he bent the sticks into position. As Father approached within a few feet of the first well, the top of the stick started to very slowly turn downward, the "V" portions of the stick rotating in his hands. He turned toward the other well and as he approached within one foot of the well the top part of the stick very slowly started to bend downward, stopping only after bending about three inches. Father chuckled a little and shook his head and he began to walk across the property near the Ollis home, stick held upward. This went on for twenty minutes with the stick doing nothing but sticking straight up. Father then began walking as far away as he could from the creek area, constantly turning on his heel left and then right, witching the area as he walked.

"Fred," Brother Ollis called out. "I don't think there will be any water over where it is dry. The well drillers said that there was no water to be found in that area." Father ignored Brother Ollis and continued to walk toward the most unlikely place for a well on the property that was still reasonably close to the house. I stayed as close as possible to Father, watching his every move. The August heat was now causing sweat to drip down his forehead onto his nose. Father approached the rocky, dusty, dry area of the field where it looked like nothing had grown in decades. Suddenly, the top part of the stick immediately went straight down toward Father's feet. It was amazing; it did not move slowly, but went straight down as if it was falling off a steep cliff. I had seen Father do this before but never saw the stick move so quickly. Father walked about fifteen feet away from the point, put his stick into the upright position and started to walk toward the same dry area. Again the stick pulled down as fast as a speeding rocket. Father put his right foot out and with his boot made an "X" in the dirt. He walked a few feet, bent over, and picked up a large rock and set it in the middle of the "X". By this time Brother Ollis had caught up to us. Father turned to Vern and said in a low but serious tone.

"Vern, have them dig your well exactly there, not here." Father pointed about a six inches away from the middle of his "X". "Not there," pointing the other direction. "But right here." Again Father pointed at the middle of the "X" with the "V" end of his willow branch.

Father motioned with his head throwing it from left to right. "Freddie, come here and take the willow." I sheepishly grabbed the willow from Father.

"Now step about five feet away and hold the willow as I have shown you."

I took the willow "V" portion in both hands and slowly bent the branches with the longer portion of the willow straight up as if pointing at my chin. I began to walk toward the "X" and when I was within a foot of the "X," the willow branch pulled straight down, twisting in my hands so fast that I couldn't hold the branches in my hand without them twisting. I stepped back and approached the "X" again, re-adjusting the willow branch pointing upward. This time I held the branches as tight as possible as I walked toward the "X". Within a few seconds the tightly held branches twisted in my hands as the top of the willow, quickly and forcefully, pulled straight down to the ground right on top of the "X".

Brother Ollis stood there and watched me with amazement, just shaking his head. "Can I try for a minute?" he asked.

Father reached over and grabbed the willow stick from my hands, then turned to Brother Ollis. "Just drill there, Vern, and you will be fine. Now we have to be going." Father began to walk away from Brother Ollis, waving with his right hand while holding his trusty willow branch by his left side.

"Thank you, Fred. I really appreciate it!" Brother Ollis shouted as we walked away. Father gave another wave of his right hand not breaking his stride or turning to look at Brother Ollis behind us. I hurried to keep up with Father's long stride.

Just after crossing the stream Father turned to me with a slight smile. "Never give your stick to a non-believer, Freddie." Father then took the stick in both hands and broke it in two, throwing one piece of the willow branch in one direction and then the other piece of willow stick in the other direction.

It was early in the afternoon and Father was walking faster, trying to get home in time for a late lunch. I could barely keep up, every once in awhile running for a second or two to stay beside Father.

As we were nearing home, and I came running up just past him, I turned and said, "Father, did you ever go exploring with your friends in Lake County where it was really scary?"

"What do you mean son?" Father asked without slowing or taking his eyes off the dirt road.

"Well, you know up on the ridge where the railroad tracks are…."

Father interrupted me and began to noticeably slow his stride. He turned to me with a stern look. "I thought I told you not to go up there."

"Oh no," I exclaimed. "I wasn't asking if I could go up there. I was just wondering if you heard anything about the ranch just over the hill from the ridge."

"What ranch?" Dad began to pick up his pace again, road dust puffing up from his shoes with each step.

"Bickford Ranch," I exclaimed with a slight voice of excitement. "You know the real big ranch?"

Father shook his head slowly left and right. "I don't know what you are talking about, but wherever this ranch is, you stay away. Ranchers around here are rumored to shoot trespassers first and then ask questions later."

I nodded my head in agreement and didn't say anything else. I did not want to tip off Father that we were thinking of exploring the abandoned ranch.

CHAPTER TEN
THE OLLIS WELL

I later learned the following story from the Ollis boys, Lane and Deon. Back at the Ollis house that afternoon, Lane and Deon were standing next to their father eyeing the big "X" mark in the dirt.

"So he said this was the place to dig for a well?" Lane asked, laughing under his breath. Lane was the oldest boy, a 14 year old soon to be a freshman in high school and clearly the leader among the children at home. He was average height for a boy of his age but had a noticeably stocky build. His broad shoulders and large arms made him look like a lumberjack. He had a very prominent square jaw with high cheek bones and deep set blue eyes. He combed his thick dark black hair over to the side of his forehead, yet leaving it long on the sides so that you could only see half of his ears. Deon was thirteen years old and a slender lanky lad with dark brown hair and a long pointed nose. He had sharper features than his brother and a very broad smile. It was a wonder that they were even brothers.

Deon was quiet like his dad, but Lane was bold and opinionated. Lane openly questioned whether or not they should listen to Fred Nickel and take the chance to drill in an area that the well drillers said water would not exist. Deon, however, had not said a word and was unusually quiet that evening, just standing off and observing. The boys soon went to bed.

Deon had, since he was really little, sleep walked, and his parents would always have to lock the doors at night and would often catch him attempting to leave the house while walking in his sleep. The next morning (the day after looking at the "X"), Deon had slept in, tired from a busy day of working around the ranch. At around 8:45 a.m. Sister Ollis had made the usual large hearty breakfast of waffles and eggs. With the exception of Deon and his younger brother and sister, everyone was at the breakfast table enjoying their morning meal. The large round table sat in the center of the raised nook next to the large spacious kitchen. A large rectangular window adorned the nook, affording a beautiful view of the family garden and woods just beyond the ranch. Deon slowly made his way up the three stairs that lead to the dining nook. He was wearing blue and white flannel pajamas that were well worn past their time. After pausing for just a second, Deon walked over next to his sister Kendra who was in the process of enjoying pouring the hot syrup over her steaming waffles. Deon turned toward Kendra's chair, bent over slightly and then with both hands pulled down his pajamas and underwear and began to pee on Kendra's chair. She shrilled and jumped out of her chair as Deon continued to pee on her chair. Brother Ollis leaped from his chair and grabbed the back of both of Deon's shoulders yelling "Wake up son, wake up!" Deon was immediately startled and jumped back.

"Huh, huh, what is it, what is wrong?" he said while now only slightly dripping pee on the urine soaked dining room chair. Deon, realizing that his pajamas were down, finally came to his senses and pulled up his underwear and pajamas and ran to the bathroom.

Kendra gasped, "You idiot!" as she looked at her left leg that she now realized was covered with urine. "That kid is gross! Why don't you put diapers on him! He's only thirteen years old!" Kendra stomped off to her room that was up a small flight of stairs.

Now, most of the family stood up and left the table, having lost their appetites. However, Lane, sitting next to the urine soaked chair, went ahead and finished the last of his syrup and butter laden waffle. "Mom are there anymore waffles?"

Later that day standing next to the "X" on the ground, Brother Ollis nodded his head and spoke to his boys. "Well, I think I will listen to Fred; I will order the well drillers in early this week and see if we strike it rich."

Two days later the drillers arrived for a third time. The Ollis family was really feeling the pinch of having to pay for drillers to come out three times. Living on a teacher's salary with a houseful of children did not afford the Ollis family the luxury of throwing money away. The large drilling truck could barely fit under the overhanging trees as it crossed the narrow bridge over the creek. It took the men at least fifteen minutes to back the truck in next to the "X".

A tall older man, who clearly had not shaven that morning, hopped out of the passenger side of the big rig and pulled out a cigarette from his brown, plaid, short sleeve shirt pocket. He reached into his right pants pocket, pulled out a Zippo lighter, flicked it and bent over and lit the cigarette. Brother

Ollis approached.

"So you think this is a good diggin place?" the man said as he blew out his cigarette smoke into Brother Ollis's face.

Brother Ollis winced and turned away slightly to avoid the smoke. "Well, my neighbor Fred Nickel from up the road witched this spot and told me this would be the best place to dig."

The gruff old man, probably in his early 60's, was the individual that had come out on the two prior occasions and witched the area with two "L" shaped quarter inch copper rods. He held one in each hand and would wait until they crossed to designate the spot that he believed would yield a good well. The man turned and took a step back to his truck, grabbing the two metal rods that were lying on the floor of the truck.

"No." Brother Ollis replied. "There is no need for those; I am digging here right on the "X" no matter what. You will just be wasting your time."

The man paused, shook his head and turned back toward the floor of his truck, muttering curse words.

"Suit yourself. What did the other guy use? Some willow stick or something?" the man said as he began to put his gloves on. The two other workers turned and laughed while still holding their cigarettes in their lips.

"Why, as a matter of fact, he did," Brother Ollis replied eagerly.

The gruff man finished putting his gloves on and walked past Brother Ollis toward the back of the rig. "Old wives' tale, that's all it is. It's your money, not mine," he mumbled as he passed by.

Brother Ollis had brought a chair that he placed far enough away from the workers so as not to bother them, yet close enough so that he could see the drill penetrating the ground. He had brought a brown one gallon thermos with him and set it beside his chair on the dusty ground. After a good half hour of preparations, the drilling rig was ready to go. The tall drilling tower was in position and looked awkwardly out of place among the beautiful forested property.   As the drill first penetrated the ground a large puff of dust billowed above the hole. Within a minute the dust had cleared and a visible hole was being made with the four inch drilling head and shaft. The workers had twenty foot drilling shafts attached to the drill head and would have to stop and add a shaft every half hour or so depending upon what type of material they were hitting in the hole.

Though sitting under a small tree in the field, the heat was beginning to cause Brother Ollis to perspire. Small beads of sweat were forming on his nose and forehead. He nervously opened up his thermos, tipped his head back, placed the small round mouthpiece on his lips and took a long drink, water spilling out the sides of his mouth and onto his shirt. He mumbled a prayer, "Lord please help them hit water soon." Time passed. Brother Ollis knew that he was charged per foot, not by the job, and the deeper they drilled, the more expensive it got. He knew that five drilling shafts had been already placed into the well and they were now working on the sixth. That meant that the drillers would reach 120 feet after this last shaft. No water had come up yet, just dry dirt and rocks from the well-head area. Worry consumed Brother Ollis. The last two wells had at least showed wet dirt by 100 feet. They were now almost at 120 feet without water in sight.

The old, gruff well driller walked over to Brother Ollis. As he approached, Brother Ollis stood up from his chair and wiped his sweat laden brow with the back of this left hand. The man had an obvious smirk on his face.

The man took off his red Larry Tanko hat and with a nod of his head and slight smile looked at Brother Ollis square in the eyes. "Well, we will be approaching 140 feet soon. How far do you want to go?" He paused then, seeing that Brother Ollis was thinking. "We can dig all day if you want and see if we can find gold or maybe even oil." His chest raised and head tilted back as he chuckled. Now his smile was wider and broader than ever and you could clearly see the nicotine and coffee stained crooked teeth.

Brother Ollis looked stern and lifted his head slightly. "Just keep going, I will tell you when to stop."

"Okay with me," the man said as he put his hat on his head. He turned to his left quickly and began walking toward the rig. Brother Ollis followed a few paces behind the man, curious to see the operation up close. As he approached the rig, the noise level was surprisingly fairly low. Brother Ollis could feel the ground rumble as he grew closer to the spot where the well was being drilled. He stopped at the edge of the large pile of dry dirt that was slowing piling up. The expression on his face told all; he knew he could not go much farther without breaking the family financially. They were at the end of another twenty-foot shaft. One of the men turned down the idle and began to prepare the rig for another twenty-foot section. The grumpy old man was now clearly happy that a local farmer was not able to find water when a crazy neighbor told him to drill a spot found by using a stupid willow stick. He stepped away from the drill and turned to Brother Ollis.

"Sir," he said while bobbing his head slowly up and down with a smile. "I told you this hole would not get you anything. Shall we patch her up?" Brother Ollis was ready to cry; he tightened his throat in attempt to stop the tears from flowing, but one slowly dripped out of the corner of his right eye.

He straightened. "No, put on one more stick and that will be all."

"Ok, if you just want to keep throwing money away that is fine." The smile became noticeably wider on the man's face and the other two men working closer to the rig were clearly laughing and shaking their heads side to side.

After about ten minutes the men had the other twenty foot pipe loaded and ready to dig deeper. As the motor on the rig was revved up the men began to get the drill going. The now grumpy Brother Ollis stepped closer to the drill and dangerously peeked over a small barrier on the side of the rig to look at the hole. No sooner than he began to lean, the drill surged and bounced, causing the drilling rig to lean forward, then back. The drill was now drilling at a considerably slower rate, probably at half speed. The drill shook again after only a few more inches of depth. Brother Ollis, still looking like a grumpy old man, leaned over again dangerously close to the drill that was now clearly straining to get through something.

"Must be hitting a rock," one worker yelled over the noise of the rig to the grumpy old man. Brother Ollis nodded and leaned over the safety barrier just a little more when a loud "boom" sounded and water sprayed directly up around the drill and out of the hole. It was like a geyser had just gone off at Yellowstone. The water pressure was so intense that it blew the hat right off Brother Ollis. The water was spraying all over the rig and the workers near by. The workers and Brother Ollis just stood there for a second in awe as the water soaked everyone within a few feet of the rig.

"I'll be," said Brother Ollis, shaking his head left and right, no longer looking grumpy.

Brother Ollis was close enough that the spray from the geyser was landing on his head. He shook his head left and right, putting his palms up and arms out in front of him while tipping his head back, soaking in the cool water drops landing on his face and hands. No one could notice the tears streaming down his cheeks as the water from the well covered his face. "Thank you Lord, thank you," he whispered quietly.

Chapter Eleven
Back to the Ridge

I t had been a couple of days since the well drillers were at the Ollis's house. The Ollis boys had not met the rest of the Penryn gang, so we all agreed to meet at the Ollis' ranch in the forested area next to the Toothly's. Scott and I now called the Toothly ranch, "Rabbit Quinten Death Row." The rabbits in the top row of cages were the rabbits next to be sacrificed for the Toothly dinner table. I wondered if Brother Toothly would come at me with a knife if I opened all the cages late one evening and freed the poor bunnies.

It was early in the morning around 9:00 a.m. Well, it was early for young boys on summer vacation. All the Penryn boys arrived at the designated spot. It was Dwayne, Owen, Stewart, Scott, Deon, Lane, and me. David and Floyd were still playing around and Scott and I refused to wait for them. We were all standing on the dirt road covered with pot holes that divided the Ollis and Toothly property. I quickly introduced everyone to the new Ollis boys who just raised their hands slightly and bowed their heads as I told them each one of the boy's names. Just as I finished introducing the last boy we heard something coming from down the road close to our property. I heard it again but this time it was much clearer and resonated with a higher pitch.

"Yeeeelllllpppppp."

I turned in unison with the rest of the boys to look down the long road. We could see a tall, lanky boy walking our way just coming out of the shadows of the trees that lined the road.

"Yeeeellllppppp."

The sound was coming from the boy walking down the road. This time he waived his right hand high in the air, waving it back and forth. "Yeeeellllpppp."

The boy approached; he was even taller up close. He was no older than thirteen or fourteen but must have been at least six feet tall. He was wearing navy blue slacks that were tightly buttoned up around his belly button. The bottoms of his pants were a good six inches higher than the top of his shoes. This boy clearly must have been growing like a weed and his parents could not keep him in pants that fit him.

His hair was dark, straight and looked wet, matted over to one side of his head. His hair looked like Alfalfa's from the Little Rascals, but he did not have the single strand of hair sticking up in the back. He wore the typical lightweight flannel, checkerboard looking short sleeve shirt that we all wore. His shoes looked like they were the size of a man, seeming to be almost twice as big as mine.

No one said anything as he approached, hand still slightly raised. He stopped and smiled broadly, causing his snow-white cheek bones to raise and almost close his eyes. Everyone still stared. Stewart looked at him curiously, turning his head left and then right, chin up and then down as if eyeing the boy's clothing. I wondered if Stewart was admiring his unusual pants. For the first time Stewart was wearing normal 501 blue jeans with the exception of both front pockets intentionally being ripped halfway down, laying open so one could see the inside top part of the pockets.

Stewart finally piped up. "What's up with the floods?"

You see, Stewart's pants usually barely fit on the lower part of his waist and always seemed to be longer than his legs. The bottom portion of his pants always looked like an accordion because they were too long.

"What?" the tall young boy exclaimed as he looked down toward his shoes. He then looked up with a stern look. "These are not floods." Just then another smaller boy came running up to us from the same direction. I was so affixed on the tall young boy that I did not even notice the other boy until he was right upon us. He was clearly the brother of the other boy, almost an identical twin with only two exceptions. First, he was much younger and shorter. Second, though of the same color and material, his pants were at least ten inches above the top of his shoes.

The young boy stopped right next to his brother and smiled.

Stewart turned and looked at him and jerked back as if he had just happened upon a rattlesnake and pointed at the younger boy's pants. "No, you are right! Now those are what I call floods!"

The boys all started to snicker, and Scott, not able to hold it, bent over laughing so hard that spit began drooling out of his mouth and other fluids began coming out of his nose. The new, younger brother stood there without a clue as to what everyone was laughing about.

Stewart turned back away from the two new boys and continued his conversation with us. "Soooo, what do you guys want to do?"

Everyone paused; Lane, raising his hand half way began to mutter, "Well, I was thinking we should build a tree fort that we could call 'The Penryn Boys Tree Fort.' I have found the perfect tree that is strong and tall." Lane turned on his heel half way and pointed with his right toward the worn pathway leading to the thickly forested area of his ranch.

I, along with the others, bent our heads slightly over and squinted our eyes in order to pick out the tree he was referring to.

"Can't you see it, the big one?" Lane said while beginning to raise his right hand and finger higher than before.

"What, you mean the tree over there, the tallest one?" Scott asked sheepishly.

"Yes," Lane said. "That's the one. We can build the fort up in between those three large forks up high in the tree," Lane continued. "I figured out that we could nail thirty two to thirty four wooden steps, one feet apart, to reach the area of the tree where we could start nailing our first two by four."

The tree Lane was referring to was by far the largest tree in the forested area. It looked like a large tall redwood with branches the size of many tree trunks. However, knowing that there were no redwoods in this area, I was resigned to the fact that I did not care what type of tree it was, but that it was just huge.

Stewart stepped forward even closer to the middle of the circle of boys. "Let's talk about the tree fort later. I want to go to Bickford Ranch and see what is up there."

Dwayne immediately shook his head and raised his right hand, palm facing Stewart and turned to walk away, mumbling, "Nope, not for me."

"What's wrong, Dwayne?" Stewart exclaimed. Still shaking his head, Dwayne muttered, "Nothing, I just think it's a bad idea to hang out with the spooks at Bickford Ranch. And I'm not feeling up to being killed and thrown down one of those Bickford caves."

Lane cocked his head and turned quickly toward Dwayne. "What caves?"

Dwayne gave Lane a puzzled look. "You know, the Bickford Ranch and all the mining caves on the ranch."

"You mean, like real mines and real caves?" Lane asked in an excited tone.

"No, the fake ones," Dwayne answered in a smart alec way, shaking his head back and forth.

I butted in. "We're not going up there. My dad would kill me if he knew we were going to the ranch. Besides, if old farmer Shepman is crazy, I bet any rancher on spooky Bickford is even crazier."

Suddenly from behind me I heard the new boy exclaim, "I'm in for going! That sounds fun."

Stewart sighed. Being the dare devil of the Penryn boys, he did not want to seem at all like a coward, especially to the new flood pants boys. "I'm for it; we've got all day to get there, explore and get back."

Scott shook his head, as he was always the one that had more common sense than all of us boys combined. "I think I'll stick around here."

Dwayne just kept shaking his head and not responding.

I pondered what I wanted to do. Truthfully I could not wait to go explore Bickford Ranch, but I clearly did not want to get in trouble with Dad. I knew that a lickin' from him would be imminent if he found out that I went to Bickford Ranch. I was in a daze sitting there, contemplating my decision when I heard another familiar voice.

"Hey guys, what's going on?"

I looked behind me and Owen was walking toward us with his usual Owen walk. His walk was one that was hard to describe because it was so unique that I don't believe anyone could describe such a walk without actually seeing it. It was almost like a penguin walk with longer steps. He was a very skinny, long lanky-arm boy. When he walked, his arms swung like a monkey taking long slow strides. He was always in a slight hunched over position with head and chin protruding out unusually far in front of his body.

"Hey Owen," a few boys replied.

The two new boys were still standing by, not saying much. All the boys, including myself, were ignoring them, still talking amongst ourselves, trying to figure out what we should do.

Finally I decided. "I'm going with you guys. I...."

Owen interrupted. "Going where?"

"To Bickford Ranch," Stewart replied.

"Okay, sounds good to me!" Owen exclaimed as he bobbed his head up and down. Owen turned to me, leaning over toward my ear. "Say, who are the dorks with floods?"

"I don't know—guess they're some new kids whose family is building a house above the hill from our house." Owen just rocked back and forth as he nodded, bottom lip protruding out beyond his upper lip.

One of the new boys piped up. "Hey, I think there is a quicker way to get up to the ridge from my property." Glancing at each other, we all shrugged our shoulders and turned to follow the two new kids that wore flood pants. They both smiled, clearly happy that they could be of some assistance to our little group, hoping that this would allow them to be accepted as part of the gang.

As we walked down the dusty, old dirt road we came upon the back side of our property. I could see Floyd again playing next to the tree by the garage. As soon as we were close to our pasture fence, Scott grabbed the new wooden railing, stepped up onto the bottom rail and leaped over the fence into our pasture. "So long suckers!" Scott exclaimed, waving with his right hand as he walked away.

By this time we had learned that the older floodpants boy was named Ron Yelper. Then, a beautiful, young male black lab came trotting down the hill toward us. Ron clapped his hands together and leaned over. "Come here Zeke a Deke." The dog's tail began to wag furiously causing his hind-quarter to wiggle left to right as he approached us. He was a husky ninety-pound dog that clearly came from a stocky line of Labs. Zeke licked Ron's face with his slobbery tongue. No sooner than he did that, Bear came barreling from our field, running under the lower wooden fence rail and under the barbed wire, wagging her tail as she ran to greet Zeke. They stopped side by side, each turning to sniff each other's butt, tails straight up and partially wagging while performing the typical dog greeting.

We continued walking down the narrow rut-filled dirt road that separated the Yelper and Nickel ranches. After their greeting, Bear and Zeke bolted toward a large pond off to our right that lay next to the dusty road. Numerous trees surrounded the pond and the shores were full of cattails. Upon reaching the edge of the pond, I stepped off of the road to the edge and reached for a cattail. The cattail tops were large, brown hot dog shaped tops and were perfect for breaking. I snapped off three of the largest cattails near me. Each boy then stepped over next to me and followed suit. The dogs frolicked in and around the pond for a few seconds, causing a pair of mallard ducks to fly away quacking a few feet over our heads. More than likely these ducks were headed over to Grandma and Grandpa's pond, two ranches over.

The road forked with one fork going straight toward the Yelper house and the other turning to the right leading the way to the end of the Yelper property. I had never been this far up the road and now could see in the distance that the dirt road lead to an old barbed wire gate. Just then I heard Ron's brother, John, yelling, "Stop it you idiot!"

I turned to my left and Ron was hitting John with the top of a cattail, causing the white and brown fuzzy material to explode into the air as the top of the cattail broke open. Soon I got hit with a cattail which caused the white and brown fuzzy material to billow into my hair and onto my clothes. Soon all the boys were pounding each other with the cattails, causing large clouds of cattail fuzz to billow all around the road. One cattail exploding onto one's body would cause millions of fuzzy particles to go everywhere. Now that ten or twelve of them were being used as weapons, it looked as if we were in a war-zone of cattail fuzz.

After the cattail war, we continued to walk up the dirt road with Stewart and Lane throwing the last of the cattails on the ground before reaching the barbed wire gate. An old tree-lined dirt road ran parallel to the fence line of the Yelper ranch and once the barbed wire gate was undone, we were on the road. Straight ahead was a very large field, maybe eighty acres in total, filled with cattle. To the left the road went steeply down the hill and out of sight. To our right the thick trees almost completely covered the top of the road making the road look like a tunnel. Lane stepped ahead of all of us who were just staring ahead at the field. Ron was in the back trying to put the barbed wire gate back into place. For some reason no one had brought their BB guns this time and I thought to myself that it would be almost worth running back home for my gun. Afraid of being left behind, it did not take long for me to change my mind and stay with the group. Ron turned back toward us, pointing straight toward the field and into the air.

"See that up there? This is the short-cut to the ridge. It's a harder climb, but it should take us no more than thirty minutes."

While listening to Ron, the first bead of sweat rolled down my face, bringing my mind back to the last time I hiked up toward the ridge when a seemingly easy hike turned very difficult. And again, like last time, I forgot to bring water. The last time we drank the ditch water both Scott and I sat over the toilet throwing up the next morning. I must have thrown up two or three times. It was obvious that our sickness was from the water we drank out of the ditch that hot August day.

Ron leaned down, lifted two of the four barbed wires with his hands, and stepped through the fence, getting the back of his shirt caught on one of the barbs, but he got through. Each boy did the same, reaching for the top strand of barbed wire with one hand while pushing the lower strand down with another while leaning through. The dogs would just run through like no barbed wire existed, getting tangled up only for a moment before forcing their way through.

Our group of boys, being so large this time, seemed more likely to be spotted as we began to walk across the large open grass field that sat at the base of the large ridge. However, though a small wooden cabin stood nearby, there was no one within a half of a mile of our path. Boy, the country was sure remote and beautiful; we had no problems worrying about getting hit by a car on the street or seeing large groups of kids ready to look for any reason to fight, like in the city. The thick, dry but low-cut grass made a snapping sound each time I took a step. It was obvious that cattle had eaten the grass down just a few inches above the ground. Both Zeke and Bear frolicked in the field, chasing every butterfly and bug that flew close to the ground. It was a pleasure to see my dog run and enjoy herself so much. Only here could dogs be allowed to run so freely without complaints from neighbors. However, Brother Toothly did mention that Bear had been over to his house a number of times, sitting outside the rabbit coup licking her lips and chomping her teeth, waiting for the opportune time to strike at the poor, helpless, innocent bunnies. But was this any crueler than Brother Toothly chopping off their heads with an axe? At least if Bear wanted to kill a bunny, she could not open the cage.

Fortunately the day was not as hot as the other time that we had hiked up to the ridge. We were able to cross the field with ease, taking about twenty-five to thirty minutes as Ron predicted. As we reached the base of the ridge, it was soon evident that though the short cut through the field was shorter than the previous one, the hike from the bottom of the ridge to the railroad tracks would not be easy. The hill was covered with thick underbrush and trees. I could not see any visible paths going straight up the bush and tree covered hill. Worst of all, I noted the three-leafed bush with reddish green leaves was scattered throughout the hill. Yes, poison oak. And today I was smart enough to wear my shorts.

I was the second one behind Ron to reach the hill and after a few seconds I could hear Dwayne and Stewart approaching, talking to one another in a gleeful tone. They immediately stopped talking when they arrived to see what I was looking at. The rest of the boys were still some 100 feet back, lagging behind.

"We're not climbing up that!" Stewart exclaimed behind me in an agitated tone.

Ron turned back, now facing Dwayne, Stewart, and me. "Why not? I've done it before."

"For one reason, there is poison oak all over the place; that is why not."

Ron furrowed his eyebrows. "Oh, you just walk through it and as soon as we get up top we jump in the water canal and wash off. Then you won't get poison oak."

Stewart, Dwayne and I slowly shook our heads back and forth with eyebrows furrowed.

"You've got to be kidding me," I stated.

"No, it really works," Ron stated with more fervor.

Just then, I looked to my left and saw Bear and Zeke playing in the bushes of poison oak, leaning and laying up against the bushes as if to scratch their sides and backs.

Stewart turned heel to his left and started to walk. "I don't know about you guys, but I am going to find another way."

"Suit yourself," Ron said as he began to walk through the thick bushes.

Right about then, Lane and Deon approached.

"What's all the fuss about?" Lane asked.

"All this has to do about nothing!" I exclaimed.

"Where is Stewart going?" Deon asked, as he pointed his finger in Stewart's direction.

Dwayne turned to his left and began to follow Stewart. "We are finding another way that does not have poison oak."

I followed Dwayne, but Lane and Deon just stood there.

As I turned after walking a few feet to my left, I could see Lane and Deon shrug their shoulders and follow in step behind Dwayne and me.

No more than five minutes later we found a well worn open path that meandered straight up the side of the ridge.

"Aha!" Stewart exclaimed, bouncing his head up and down while cracking a smile. "I knew there had to be a better way."

We followed behind as Stewart began walking semi-hunched over to get traction up the steep, dusty, slippery switchback. After an hour or so of hiking since we had left for the ridge, I was beginning to feel thirsty from the 90 to 100 degree weather. I looked at my dust covered, black Converse high tops as I trudged up the hillside following closely behind Stewart with Dwayne close behind me. I paused to look back and saw Lane and Deon were not far off, though clearly becoming more winded as time went on. After about fifteen more minutes of hiking, I could see the first tier of the ridge appear where the railroad tracks ran. There was still the very large hill on the other side of the railroad tracks that lead to Bickford Ranch. This hill was at least two or three times higher than the hill that we had just traversed.

We finally reached the top of the first hill where it flattened out to the railroad tracks. I looked back to the east and noticed that we were no more than 100 yards from where we came up on the previous ridge hike. It sure seemed like an awful lot of work for saving only a few yards of walking. As I scanned back to my left, breathing a heavy sigh to catch my breath, I noticed a figure moving just on the other side some twenty feet or so above the railroad tracks near the irrigation ditch. Sure enough it was Ron, soaking wet from head to toe, shaking his head like a dog to get all of the water off of his face and out of his hair. He continued twice to shake his head like a dog before beginning to walk towards us. By this time Lane and Deon were just cresting the hill, huffing, puffing and sweating. Lane leaned over and placed his hands on his knees, attempting to catch his breath. He straightened up, squinted his weary eyes open, and peered toward Ron.

"What is he all wet from?" he said, continuing to peer at Ron.

Dwayne chuckled. "I guess he had to take a bath in the ditch to clean off the poison oak."

"What poison oak?" Lane asked in great panic.

"The poison oak that we did not go through." Stewart answered.

"Oh," Lane stated with a sigh of relief. "I had poison oak once so bad that I could hardly move. It started on my hands and for some reason then broke out on my crotch area. Boy was that miserable." Lane shook his body and head left to right to emphasize his displeasure with the memory.

Ron approached the rest of us, dripping from head to toe. "That water felt good-- had to get the poison oak off my body. You guys might want to do it just in case."

"Thanks, but no thanks," Dwayne replied, half chuckling.

"Well, what are we all standing here for? Let's get going," Stewart stated with urgency in his voice.

It was getting hotter by the minute and the dripping water from Ron looked cool and refreshing. The fact that I had no hat on was causing me to become more dehydrated and I began to wonder if I could take a drink of water out of the ditch without getting sick. Then, flashing back to the toilet, I threw the stupid idea out of my mind.

We all walked in almost single file westward toward the large Clark Train Tunnel. The tracks ran along side us to the right with the ditch full of water on the opposite side of the track, slightly up the hill. I kept peering over toward the ditch, seeing every few feet glimpses of the top of the cement ditch through the grass. We were no more than 100 yards from the final bend in the tracks and hills before reaching the tunnel, but I could not stand it anymore. Sweat was now pouring down my face, dripping in my eyes every couple of minutes.

"Hey, stop you guys!" Ron and Stewart were in front and the rest of us were in the back.

"Let's take just a minute and climb up the hill and jump in the irrigation ditch." Everyone stopped and paused for a few seconds and then Dwayne bolted from behind me, jumped over the railroad tracks and ran at full speed up the fairly steep hill on the other side of the tracks. Stewart, Lane and I followed suit until all of us were running up the hill at full speed. Bear and Zeke had already passed all the boys and were three-fourths of the way up the hill. The run up the hill took no more than two or three minutes and then we were standing on top looking down at the railroad tracks below. The hill must have been 100 feet above the railroad tracks. I could hear the trickling of the ditch water and turned to see Bear and Zeke jumping in and out of the ditch.

Dwayne was the first one to jump into the ditch followed by me, Lane and Stewart. Soon all boys and dogs were in the ditch splashing and frolicking in the cool water. Cool drops of water now replaced the hot drips of sweat previously running down my cheek. We stayed in the ditch for at least five minutes, sitting, standing and splashing in the water. I stepped out dripping from head to toe. Slowly all the boys stepped out of the ditch, not an easy task with soaking wet Levi jeans. The two dogs were the only ones that refused to get out of the cool water of the ditch.

Dripping wet, standing next to the ditch, Lane turned to his right. "Hey, let's get some rocks to block the ditch and make a pool so we can do some cannon balls and swim. I paused, nodding my head up and down, lips tight together.

"Sounds like a good idea to me." I jumped across the ditch and walked ten or twelve feet up the hill and found a large, thirty to forty pound moss rock. I grunted as I lifted it and turned to my right, both hands hanging down near my waist with the rock cradled in my hands against my stomach. Slowly walking to Lane who was in the ditch, I leaned over and handed it to him. Just then, Dwayne approached with a rock that weighed at best five to ten pounds.

"I need a bigger rock than that!" Lane exclaimed.

Dwayne paused and looked with puzzlement at Lane. "What, that is a big rock, what to you want me to do, kill myself?"

Lane shook his head and continued carefully placing the rocks in a straight line across the ditch to form a dam. Each boy continued carrying rocks to Lane. The water slowly began to build with just small amounts of water coming through the cracks in between the rocks. The water began to rise steadily until it was up to Lane's waist. The rock wall, neatly stacked, began to rise steadily as we worked until the water was up past Lane's stomach.

"It's getting close to the top; I only need three or four more rocks. Get me two big ones and one small one!" Lane shouted as he gently attempted to straighten the last few rocks on top of the wall. The pool that formed behind the carefully placed rock wall was deep enough to do a cannon ball. The water reached the top of the four-foot cement side walls of the irrigation ditch. Just a small trickle of water was flowing down the ditch behind the rock wall.

"That looks awesome," Dwayne stated as he stood with sweat dripping down each side of his face. "Can I jump in now?"

Just as Dwayne finished his statement I heard Stewart directly behind me.

"Ahhh!" Stewart yelled, running past Dwayne and me, jumping straight in the air and landing butt first into the deep pool of water. The water splashed out both sides of the ditch. Dwayne was soon followed by me, John and Ron. Lane was stomach deep in the water and was already cooled off.

This felt much better than before as the water was deeper and much cooler, covering me just past my stomach. I took my shirt off and threw it to the right side of the ditch in the now wet and slightly muddy decomposed granite along the ditch. This time the dogs hesitated to jump into the deeper water but instead chose to jump in up the canal a little farther away from the splashing and frolicking of the boys.

I stuck my head under the water, which was easy to do now that it ran deep. Stewart thought the same thing and we hit heads as we pulled out of the water.

"Dork!" Stewart yelled, using his right hand to splash me in the face.

"Dork you, pants man!" I said as I splashed him back.

Soon a full-fledged water-splashing fight erupted, and then after a few minutes of splashing, I sat down in the ditch with my hands under my butt bouncing off the bottom. The water was up to my neck and without the use of my hands would be almost over my head. I looked to my left as I enjoyed the water and noticed that the water level was now above the cement top of the ditch and was spilling over onto the decomposed granite hill and disappearing over the hill.

I thought nothing of the water slightly spilling over the hill. I was happy to be cool and I was enjoying our homemade swimming pool. After fifteen minutes, each boy began to step out of the homemade pool, dripping wet. Only Stewart, Lane and I had taken our shirts off and now had to take them and dip them in the water to clean them off from the decomposed granite mud.

Stewart had a stick in his hand, and standing next to the ditch where the water was slowly over-flowing the sides, said "Yes, master we will produce a waterfall, one greater than the earth has ever seen." Stewart then proceeded to take the sharp end of the stick and place it on the ground and pull it away from the ditch forming a small furrow in the dirt. I grabbed a small branch that had fallen from an oak tree some twenty feet away and ran back to help Stewart.

"Yes, we will make the greatest waterfall that mankind has ever known. They will call us great and wonderful and praise our name as the creators of the Penryn waterfall."

I began to help Stewart carve out a furrow that began from the edge of the irrigation ditch to the edge of the mountainside. About 100 feet below the ditch was the railroad tracks where our waterfall ended its journey.

No sooner than we were finishing up with our great creation, I heard a rattle to my right and Bear and Zeke barking madly as if they were in serious trouble. I dropped my stick and ran toward the dogs that had their heads held high and tails straight up near the old oak tree where I found the stick. Stewart was right beside me when I noticed a large six-foot rattlesnake coiled up ready to strike at the dogs. I grabbed Bear by her tail and pulled her backwards so that neither I, nor she, would be bitten. The snake continued to rattle, but still did not strike at Zeke who was still taunting the snake. Holding Bear with my right hand, I reached for Zeke's tail but then Ron grabbed Zeke by the hind legs and pulled him back from the snake. Bear continued to struggle in attempt to free herself from my grip of her tail. She turned and flailed toward me, attempting to bite my hand. As she turned I was able to grab her collar and drag her further away from the rattlesnake. Lane and Dwayne approached with large rocks in their hands.

"Die like a bug, you sucker!" Lane shouted, as he hurled a ten-pound rock onto the snake. The rattlesnake twisted in pain as Dwayne hurled another rock striking the snake directly on the top of the head. The snake, now confused, was not sure which way to go and attempted to flee our harassment, but having been injured thought that coming toward us was getting away.

All the boys scrambled away as the snake flailed toward us in a panic. I did not care what was happening; all I thought was to get out of there as quickly as possible. I dragged Bear by the collar across the dirt and down the hill and then across the railroad tracks to a place of safety. All the other boys were scattering in different directions in attempt to get away from the angry, confused rattlesnake. Within a matter of minutes everyone had gathered at the railroad tracks just east of where the snake had been.

Dwayne was the last one to arrive, huffing and puffing and trying to say something but unable to due to the lack of oxygen. He finally managed. "Hey, let's get out of here before another snake comes after us."

By this time, Bear was calmed down enough that I could let her go and not worry about her going back to find the snake. I turned with all the other Penryn Boys and started to walk along the tracks back to our home.

"What about this Bickford Ranch?" Ron asked.

"We're not going back there to get bit by a snake now. I'll wait until another time," Stewart replied.

All the boys nodded in approval, following Stewart toward home.

The sun was starting to go down over the hill just above Clark Tunnel in the west. The view was spectacular as we walked along the ridgeline. The orangeish-red sun caused the golden brown fields in the valley to look as if the tops of the grass had a tinge of red on top. Though my stomach was gurgling from hunger, the slight summer breeze felt refreshing on my face as I slowly walked with my friends toward home.

Chapter Twelve
The Train

It was Sunday, the morning after another high adventure on the ridge. I awoke to another pheasant rooster crowing on the front lawn outside my second story bedroom window. I had slept in until 8:30 and the bright morning sunlight was shining through the crack in my curtains. I could hear stirring and movement downstairs and what appeared to be the sound of my mother's radio. Mother liked to listen to news radio on the A.M. dial so that she could work around the house and still hear the happenings of the day.

I stretched my arms, pushing the sheet off my body, and got up. As I walked to my door the board squeaked as I stepped on it near the doorway. A new home and this creaking sound was already beginning. I stepped into the doorway of Scott's room to see a neatly made bed. Floyd and Davids' rooms were also empty, but their beds were still unmade.

It was the end of August and in only a week we would be in our new school meeting new kids and, more importantly, new girls. Being the new face at school was always good as the girls tended to want new boys around. Heck, who wanted the same old guys when you could have a new one, even if he wasn't as cute as the others. I could not wait to meet Valerie Smith, the beautiful girl that all the boys had been raving about. I could imagine her long, shiny, blonde hair and her piercing blue eyes. I imagined her beautiful dimpled smile revealing her beautiful straight white teeth. If she was even half the girl that my friends described her to be, I would instantly fall in love.

I popped down the stairs like a rabbit jumping through the grass. I took two, and once, three, steps at a time, almost breaking my neck in the process. As I rounded the bottom of the stairs toward the kitchen, Mom was cooking breakfast with her usual A.M. news station on. Scott was sitting there staring at me with the look of fear. His spoon in his right hand was full of Life cereal, milk dripping from the bottom of the spoon. He quickly nodded his head twice to the right toward the radio.

"We are here, live, on the ridge near Clark Tunnel Road in Penryn," a reporter stated in an excited voice.

"The whole side of the hill has been washed away down onto the railroad tracks. I am here with Penryn Fire Chief Jed Houseman. Chief, what happened and what caused the hill to come down onto the tracks?"

By this time I was at the corner of the bar within a few feet of Scott. Scott's eyebrows raised and his lips tightened to a small circular hole. I stood there and listened as Scott continued to eat his cereal. Mom was busy cooking breakfast and doing dishes almost at the same time while listening intently. Dad was sitting at his usual seat in the nook at our small round table with his back facing the window from which one could look out to see up to the ridge. Dad's back was to the window but his head was turned to his left, bobbing up and down to get a better view out the window toward the ridge.

The fire chief replied: "well, the engineer of Train 243 came out of the tunnel pulling a full load when he noticed ahead a large dirt mound on the tracks. He attempted to stop but was unable to do so in time and struck the large pile of dirt. The train stopped and the water soaked mountain continued to come down on top of the train, causing it to become stuck."

The reporter, obviously pulling the microphone back to his mouth, asked, "What caused the mountain to become wet?"

"It was caused by vandals who had used rocks to dam up the PCWA irrigation canal, causing it to flow over the ridge and dislodge the hill."

"When did this happen?" the reporter asked.

"We are estimating sometime late yesterday afternoon or evening."

"I have here with me Placer County Sherriff Officer Ben Roach. Officer Roach do you have any suspects?"

"None at this time, but we are investigating the scene to determine who might be the perpetrators."

"Are there any signs or evidence found at the scene?"

"We have collected some evidence that we cannot disclose at this time as the investigation is ongoing. However, we did see dog tracks around the area where the ditch was dammed up with large rocks."

I knew Officer Ben Roach as he was a member of our church. He was a very well liked and respected officer that had served for many years. Ben was most well known for his service to Penryn Grammar School as a cook for the one week field trips to the coast.

Dad turned back around, picked up his fork, and began to eat the hot steaming eggs that Mom had just put in front of him. The radio was still blaring with interviews and information about the incident. Dad lifted his head from his plate and turned his head to his right where now both Scott and I were seated. I was in the middle of pouring my Life cereal.

"I sure hope I never catch you kids ever doing anything like that. I'd whip your butts so hard you would bleed for weeks."

Dad paused.

"I bet it was some out-of-town vandals that were trying to make a statement of some sort to the railroad."

Scott turned to his left and looked over at me, eyebrows lifted up in a questioning manner.

Dad had the Auburn Journal in his hands with pictures of the side of the hill piled up on the railroad track. The train was parked on either side of the tracks and one box car was high centered on the pile. He shuffled in his seat, moving the paper a bit while reading the article.

Soon the radio announcer was talking about another subject, and Dad was already past the train story, looking at the classified portion of the paper for a set of discs and spring tooth harrow for our International 300.

We arrived at church at the usual fifteen minutes earlier than the start time of 11:00 a.m. All my Penryn Boy friends were there, already preparing the Sacrament table for the blessing and passing of the Sacrament. Stewart sat quietly with his parents in a pew next to the wall. Though Willie and Jim were not at church yet, it was obvious that Stewart was going to stay close to his mom and dad and walk up to the Sacrament table to help pass the Sacrament at the last minute. Ever since that Sunday, spending the whole meeting under the Sacrament table, Stewart seemed reserved when at church.

Most of us were dressed in our white shirts with different colored, fat, short ties. It was cool to have a fat knot in the tie that did not go any further down than the middle of your torso. The style did not help those with large bellies, and it made the average guy with a normal gut look like he was pregnant. Being a little overweight and wearing a tie caused many girls to lose interest. That guy would not get a date if his life depended upon it. For this reason the Bishop had a hard time getting some kids to wear ties.

After the typical sacrament meeting of listening to adults describe stories about why we should obey the commandments, we separated to our Sunday school class. I sat next to Stewart and Owen during Sunday school, listening to a clean shaven, newly returned missionary, Brent Bosworth, teach us about something. Of course I did not know what because I was not listening. However, Brent had not lost his football body, tipping the scale at a good 225 lbs and standing a tall 6 feet 2 inches. He was one of those that would not look good in the new style tie; he was a former football player that was the teacher for our class, which had a reputation as being the rowdiest in the church. Brent was given the task of straightening up our group of rowdy boys. We were known to torture new teachers, usually ending in the teacher leaving the room in tears.

I saw Stewart carefully drawing something with a pencil on the back of the sacrament program.

"Psst! Hey check this out!" Stewart whispered.

I reached over half way between the chairs to grab what was in Stewart's hand. I could see it was some type of drawing; however, I was not sure what it was. I placed the drawing on my lap, looking down at it periodically every time Brent turned to the board to write something down that he thought was important. I saw a crude pencil drawing of what appeared to be a train with mud all over the front of it. The drawing clearly showed the rough outline of the ridgeline where the train tracks ran.

I looked over to Stewart. He was looking straight at the board where our teacher was writing scriptural references. Stewart's lips were tight together, as he clearly attempted not to laugh. His stomach heaved slightly as he still attempted to hold back the laugh. The other kids in the room looked over at him, wondering what had gotten into Stewart. He bowed his head and started to snort through his nose, still attempting to hold back from laughing out loud.

Suddenly, teacher Brent turned and sternly asked, "What is so funny Brother Toothly?"

Stewart just shook his head side to side while keeping it down toward his lap.

Unfortunately, I was so focused on Stewart that I did not notice that Stewart's crude drawing was sitting right on top of my desk in plain view. Teacher Brent took three quick steps from the chalkboard toward me, reached down and snatched the paper off my desk. I stood in disbelief.

"Hmmm, let's see what we have here," Brent stated as he peered down with squinted eyes at Stewart's crude drawing.

Just then Stewart's head came up and he turned to me and with a very scared look on his face. He made a quiet gulp.

"Brother Nickel, who drew this lovely picture?"

"Stewart did," I quickly replied

"Brother Toothly."

You see teachers would call us "Brother" when they were serious or upset at us; we were not really Brothers or Sisters in the church; we were just young kids.

"I didn't know that you were an artist," teacher Brent exclaimed as he looked up from the paper and toward Stewart. "What is this picture of?"

Stewart paused, clearly thinking what to say. He then sighed and started to explain.

"Well, you see, I like trains and mud and hills and thought that I would like to draw them. I also like guns and trees and if Fred didn't take the paper out of my hand I would have been drawing the guns and trees.

Everyone in the class looked perplexed. A number of our friends smiled and shook their heads, thinking that there is no way that teacher Brent would believe that stupid explanation.

Brent paused then shook his head up and down as he peered back at the crude drawing.

"Okay, but I spend a lot of time preparing these lessons for you kids and I expect you to pay attention." Brent then took the paper in his right hand and set it down on Stewart's table. Stewart quickly grabbed the paper, crumpled it up and put it in his front pocket. Of course, Sunday was the only day that Stewart had real front pockets in the front pocket area of his pants.

The seemingly long, boring lesson dragged on until I finally found myself in the foyer of the church looking for the rest of my family so that we could all get in the car and go home. As usual the foyer was packed with people who were mingling and visiting and talking about the day's church lessons and everyday events. I saw my mother standing outside the bishop's office with my brother's nearby. She peered at me and with her palm up motioned me to come over to her with her right finger. I slowly walked down the hall, nudging Brothers and

Sisters who were standing around, mingling, before heading home.

"Excuse me, excuse me, excuse me!" I exclaimed as I nudged and bumped into a woman standing in the hall. Sister Jones was standing between two large men and I could not quite squeeze through. I could not wait and pushed through her and another gentleman. My stomach area rubbed tightly up against Sister Jones right thigh and hip area. Sister Jones was a very attractive thirty plus year old lady. It was obvious that she did not notice the rubbing going on as she continued to talk to Brother Stoker about some problem she was having with the electrical at her house. However, to a young man this was quite a thrill, something that I would not soon forget.

By the time I reached Mom she had already struck up a conversation with Brother Bumley, an engineer with Southern Pacific Railroad. He was in his thirties and was a tall fellow, standing about 6 feet 3 inches, and was skinnier than a rail. He always hunched over a little bit when walking or when talking to someone. His brown, curly hair dangled down over his forehead to the top of his eyebrows. The sides and back of his hair was shaven military style, causing the front of his hair to appear extra long. I noticed him gesturing in an animated fashion with his hands. As I approached I could hear the conversation.

"As I came out of the Clark Tunnel," Brother Bumley stated while gesturing with his right arm moving it in a forward fashion, "I felt that something was not right. We were moving quite slow but I was pulling the hill and had a large payload. Just as I began to turn to the left around the first bend, I noticed a huge pile of wet dirt in the middle of the tracks. The pile must have been six feet high and fifteen feet wide. My eye caught water coming down the side of the mountain and a huge piece of the mountain gone."

By this time I had walked up closer where Mom, Scott, David, and Floyd were intently listening. Brother Bumley then turned to me, noticing that I was now listening to the conversation.

"I, of course, was not operating the train, as my partner Joseph was. He immediately put on the brakes attempting to stop the huge two mile long train. It threw me forward and I caught myself with this hand." Brother Bumley lifted up his left hand that had an ace bandage wrapped around it. He paused so that everyone could look at the injury and then continued.

"We were no more than 100 yards away from the huge dirt pile. I yelled at him, "Don't stop! Speed up and let the train ram through it! But he refused to listen and just kept slowing down," Brother Bumley continued, making hand and face gestures imitating those of himself and Joseph.

"I yelled at him again, "Speed up Joseph, we can make it through it." By this time I had noticed that the mountain was giving way even more and large chunks of dirt were falling down onto the tracks. As we got closer to the pile, I could see that the water was not just some little trickle but a large amount of water pouring down the mountain from what appeared to be the PCWA water ditch."

By this time a number of members of the church had gathered around Brother Bumley and were intently listening to his tale. The hall was now completely blocked and no one could get by without pushing someone out of the way. Brother Bumley noticed the crowd was getting bigger and seemed to enjoy the attention. I looked over at Scott who was not moving but was staring directly at Brother Bumley as if he was in a trance. Brother Bumley was still talking but I had zoned out for just a second, looking at the crowd that had gathered.

"We hit the pile doing about 10 mph and the train jolted and wet mud splattered all over the place. For a moment I could not see anything in front of me but spraying and spewing mud which splattered against the window, making a real loud sound. For a moment, I could not see anything as the mud completely covered both windshields. Fortunately I had the wherewithal to turn the wipers on to clean the windshield. I turned water on the windshield and eventually it was clean enough so that I could see out front.

There was that word again, "wherewithal," that the adults in Loomis and Penryn used to denote some sort of mind set. It always puzzled me, wondering what exactly that word meant.

Brother Bumley repositioned his feet and turned slightly toward me as if to address a different side of the hall. His eyes were wide open, lips tight together, preparing to continue with the story. You see, Brother Bumley was a quiet man that never drew any attention to himself. He had six small children and lived on a six acre peach ranch where he raised delicious Penryn peaches to supplement his income.

After his brief pause Brother Bumley continued. "Joseph still would not take off the brake and we finally came to a stop. I could not feel anything but feared for what had happened to the rest of the train where the mountain was coming down. You see, it took us another mile or so after hitting the mud to stop the train. After we stopped, we both paused and just looked at each other. I immediately turned toward the door of the engine, opened the door and walked down the flight of stairs."

Brother Bumley again stopped because little seven year-old, Kyle Ripson, was tugging on Brother Bumley's Coat.

"Yes Kyle?"

Kyle looked up at Brother Bumley with his big blue eyes.

"Is this a true story?"

Brother Bumley did not hesitate: "Of course it is." Slightly annoyed, Brother Bumley continued.

"I walked around the front of the train to meet up with Joseph who had already exited the train and was a few feet in front of me, walking toward the back of the train. I sped up my walk to catch up with him. We did not say anything but just walked as quickly as we could. When we finally arrived at the area of the mountain where the mud slide had occurred, I saw what I expected but hoped would not have happened. Half the mountain had now come down and had piled up against one of the box cars, causing it to be dislodged from the tracks. The car was tilted over about twenty five degrees due to the weight of the wet dirt. I stepped back because the mountain was very unstable and was still coming down onto the tracks. It was then that I noticed that the box car in front and in back of this box car had also jumped the…."

"What did you do?" Scott abruptly interrupted.

Brother Bumley now turned toward Scott to his center left and crouched down slightly.

"Well, to make a long story short, we had to call out all kinds of big tractors and unhitch the back part of the train and have another engine come up the tracks and pull all the cars back to Roseville and disconnect the front cars from the derailed box cars and pull them up to Colfax. It took all day and into the night to clean up the mess on the tracks. The railroad had to redirect trains everywhere across the West Coast because it took so long to clean up the mess and right the box cars."

Stewart Toothly's dad piped up. "Well, Jim, did you find out where the water was coming from?"

Jim nodded his head up and down quickly, lifting both eyebrows and opening his eyes wide.

"Yep. Sure did. I hiked up the hill and noticed that the PCWA ditch was dammed up with rocks. Clearly this was caused by some vandals trying to create a serious train accident. The police and railroad detectives are on the case. I guess whoever they were, they had their dog with them because there were dog prints all over the area on top of the hill."

Just then Brother Bumley's wife grabbed him by the arm in a firm grip.

"Let's go Jim. The kids are hungry and everyone is tired of hearing your story."

Brother Bumley nodded and turned to his left, walking through the crowd with his wife and six children in tow.

Chapter Thirteen
The Dark Family Plants

School was starting in a few days and the summer was coming to a close. The air was getting cooler at night and some early mornings you could see a slight glimmering dew across the grass. I decided to make one last summer pilgrimage over to Dwayne's house. It was about 8:30 a.m. and I didn't want to bother Scott to come with me. I walked out our newly graveled road that had large base rocks scattered on top of the road. The rocks made it difficult to walk as the big rocks caused me to trip every once and awhile. Halfway down the road I heard Bear come running. Within a few seconds she was at my side, nose in the dirt and tail wagging. I could never figure out why Bear always had to smell everything everywhere we went. She must have gone down this road a thousand times and still had to smell it. I could hear the small creek as I passed over the culvert in the road. Dwayne's house was just one-hundred or two-hundred yards away, but it would take a lot of hiking and climbing over a number of fences to get there.

I hesitated before reaching Dwayne's house. I was worried that Mr. Bellbuton (Dwayne's father) would be on his porch sipping his beer, holding his 30/30 rifle, and then I would have to talk to him. To my relief as I finally approached the house, I could see that no one was on the porch.

"Bam, bam, bam," the door window shook as I rapped the door. I waited for a few seconds and then I could hear someone walking across the creaky old floors. Dwayne's house was a one-hundred year old home that had been slightly, and I mean slightly, renovated. It was a small white square house with a small wooden porch out front. The only thing that looked fairly new was Dwayne's cold, dark room that was part of the old porch that had been boarded up with plywood so it could be used as a bedroom for Dwayne. The door began to open slowly, and then I noticed someone behind the door that I had never seen before. It was a girl. As the door swung wide open, I could see, through the screen door, a young girl with long brown hair. She pushed the screen door open with one hand.

"Hi, are you looking for Dwayne?"

I paused and now could see a beautiful girl without the screen hiding her. She was short with long brown hair and beautiful light brown eyes. She was wearing an old pair of Levi jeans that had a few small tears in the right knee. The tight white tank-top really looked good with the Levi's.

"Yes, yes, I'm wondering if Dwayne is around," I stuttered.

She nodded. "Sure, he's in his room. Go on back. Are you Scott?"

I didn't hesitate to reply—in fact, I think I talked over her a little bit.

"No, I'm his brother Fred."

She quickly stuck her right hand toward me and then sheepishly pulled it back.

"I'm Linda, Dwayne's sister."

"Oh," I said as I nodded my head up and down, not knowing what else to say. I just stared at her for another second, not knowing what to do next.

"Well, do you want to come in?" she asked.

"Huh?" I then looked down and noticed that I was standing over the threshold of the door, making it impossible for her to close the door.

Just then a loud yell came from the corner of the room. "Shut the damn door! You're letting in the mosquitos."

I scooted in about two feet, allowing room for Linda to close the door. It was then I noticed Mr. Bellbuton sitting in the dimly lit corner of the living room with a beer in his left hand and the daily newspaper lying on his lap. He didn't look at me, but kept his eyes down looking at the newspaper.

"Where is his room?" I asked in a quiet, subdued voice, now focusing my attention on Linda.

Pointing with her left arm extended out, Linda replied. "Over there through the kitchen."

"Thanks," I replied. The house was a very simple house but very neatly kept. I could hear music playing beyond the kitchen which became louder as I walked through and approached the only door next to the kitchen. As I reached for the knob, I could hear a Tommy Jamison and the Shandel's song called "Crimson and Clover" playing way too loud. Cracking the door, I peeked in.

"Dwayne, you there?" It was then I could see Dwayne's back with what was obviously a guitar strapped to the front of his body. He was acting like he was playing the guitar along with the song, moving his head left and right with the rhythm of the song.

'Hey," I yelled.

Dwayne jumped as if startled by a bear. He turned and looked and then took a step over to the stereo and turned down the volume, guitar still dangling from his neck.

"What's up?" Dwayne said as he turned toward me. Dwayne took off the guitar and set it in the corner of the room.

I looked around the room. It was now more obvious that it was part of the old porch that had been turned into a room. The room was no bigger than eight by eight with a single bed in the far left corner of the room and a small dresser beside it with an old clock radio on top. The carpet was old and the room was noticeably much cooler than the rest of the house.

"Is this your room?" I asked.

"Yes indeed, if you want to call it that."

"This looks like it used to be a porch."

"Yeah, when we first bought this house, my mom and dad brought us out here and gave us a tour of the new place. I was so excited to move to the country until I looked around and saw only two rooms. I looked at my parents and then my spoiled sister Linda and said to myself, "Hmm, I wonder where my room is?" Sure enough when we moved in, Dad started to board up this side of the porch.

"It seems a little cool in here," I commented.

Dwayne smiled and shook his head back and forth, "You should feel it in the winter time." Dwayne then pointed down to a small portable heater with his right hand. "But it's okay; my little heater here will handle any cold thrown at me."

The phone rang in the distance and I could hear Linda answering and then pausing. "Dwayne, phone."

Dwayne turned from me and walked out of the bedroom door toward the kitchen. I could hear Dwayne once he picked up the yellow headset.

"Yeah, what's up? Yep, he's here." There was a long pause. "Ok, meet you by the back fence of Grandma Davis."

There was another pause. Dwayne reappeared in the room. "That's Scott; he wants to meet us at Grandma Davis's backyard, and I told him we would be there in ten minutes." Dwayne barely paused to take a breath.

"Hey, you've got some baseball cards?"

"Yeah," I replied.

Dwayne nodded his head. "I have about one thousand cards. Let me show you some of my good guys that I have." Dwayne started to thumb through the messy stack of cards.

"Let's see: Boog Powell, Hank Aaron, Willie Mays, Willie McCovey, Don Sutton, Lou Brock, Harmon Killabrew and Roger Maris."

I smiled and stuck my chest out just a little. "Yeah, I have about ten thousand at my house."

Dwayne looked up from his cards. "Wow, how did you get so many?"

Just then, Mr. Bellbuton yelled from the living room. "Dwayne! Dwayne!"

Dwayne immediately dropped the cards on his bed and hurriedly went out his door. I followed right behind him, walking through the kitchen and into the living room.

"What is that dog doing on the porch?" Dwayne's dad was standing next to the window holding a rifle in his left hand, muzzle pointing down.

Dwayne and I both stopped and looked out the window on the other side of the door closest to the kitchen.

"That's my dog Bear!" I exclaimed in an excited voice. I was worried about her getting shot.

"Get the damn thing out of here!" Mr. Bellbuton shouted and then turned around and went back to his seat in the corner of the room, setting the rifle down and leaning it up against the corner of the two walls.

"We are just leaving Dad; we'll take her with us." Mr. Bellbuton didn't even acknowledge Dwayne's response.

Linda was sitting in the kitchen at the table with a sandwich in her hand. Though only a few feet away, Dwayne motioned to me with his hand to follow him. We quickly headed for the door. Just as Dwayne reached to open the door, I could hear Darla say something behind me.

"By Fred, see ya later."

I turned to see her smiling, looking straight at me, those light brown eyes piercing right through me.

I gave her a half wave with my left hand, said "Bye," and I turned and went out the door.

Dwayne was already about five steps ahead of me, so I had to pick up my walk to catch up to him. He was looking to his right toward an old wooden storage type of shed that was no larger than a small car. The vertical shaped boards were well faded, warped, and had at least a one inch gap between each board. The old wooden door was partly open and I could see a couple of men standing in the doorway.

"Yeah, looks like the neighbor Webber is here again," Dwayne stated as he shook his head and continued to walk toward the pasture.

I caught up with Dwayne and was curious what those men were doing there. Just as I was about to inquire further Dwayne continued.

"I don't know why people always want to go into that old shed. There is nothing but an old lawnmower and some garden tools in there. For some reason every time I have a friend over they want to go over and play in the old shed. I also see dad's friends out there mulling around."

"What is the big deal with the shed?" I asked curiously.

"I don't quite know why; it seems like everyone likes to hang out in there. I don't know why or what for and I really don't care."

Dwayne kept walking and didn't say anything else. As we approached the old wooden gate that connected the big yard to the pasture, Dwayne's step increased. As we approached within a foot of the gate he jumped up in the air, raised his right leg, grunted and kicked the face of the gate. The gate swung open all the way until it hit the old log and barbed wire fence with a loud bang. The old fence shook for a few seconds while Dwayne and I walked through. Dwayne just kept walking but I noticed sheep in the field and asked Dwayne, "Are you gonna close the gate?"

"Sure, go ahead."

I ran back a few feet, shut the gate, and placed the wire made like a lasso around the top of the end post to hold it secure. You see in Penryn, it seemed every gate was held by a piece of bailing wire wrapped around a fence post with a lasso style loop made to fit over the swinging gate. I guess it worked, so why do anything more? They must not have heard of latches in Penryn. I caught back up to Dwayne who was nearing one of the many big granite boulders sitting in the middle of the beautiful, green irrigated pasture.

"So what do you want to do?" I asked.

Dwayne kept walking but replied enthusiastically. "Only a few days until school starts, so I thought I would show you the Dark family's forest."

"The what?" I asked.

"The thick forested area next to the Dark's property. There are all kinds of places that you can play and explore back there."

Dwayne continued to talk about all the interesting things that might be found in the Dark's forest until we reached the back of the barbed wire fence next to Grandma Davis's house. Dwayne stepped through the second and third barbed wire, the top wire catching on his shirt, slightly tugging on it as he slithered through. He reached his hand over his back, detaching the barb from the back of his shirt. I followed. Then, within a few seconds of passing through the fence, Rusty, the Steinboton's Irish Setter, came running across the field. Rusty was a beautiful Irish Setter with long red hair that always seemed to be combed just perfectly as if he had just been given a bath and a grooming. He never barked but was always wagging his tail. He and Bear both stopped and stood tall as they met each other just on the other side of the barbed wire fence. The hair on Bear's back was raised. Within a few seconds they then decided to smell each others' butts, both with tails wagging as if to acknowledge the presence of their butts. I wondered what they might be saying to each other.

Maybe, "Hey, Bear, you haven't gone to the bathroom in days; how do you hold it so long?"

"I don't know Rusty, but it is obvious that you just took a dump a few seconds ago."

"No, Bear, that is just gas. I got so excited when I saw you that I could not help but fart."

My short, typical daydream caused me to fall a few more steps behind Dwayne.

"Come on Fred, let's get going," Dwayne yelled.

Just then I heard a noise behind me and turned to my right, noticing Dwayne's sister, Linda, following us.

"Fred, wait just a minute," she uttered while attempting to quickly slip through the barbed wire fence.

"Oh no," Dwayne uttered while shaking his head in disgust.

Linda and I soon were on Dwayne's heels, following him into what looked like a dark forest. The deep underbrush and trees allowed very little light to filter through. I could see a well worn path leading directly into the forest. As we stepped into the forest-like area known as the Dark property, Dwayne's walk noticeably slowed and he turned toward us.

"Who comes here?" I asked.

"The Darks. There are a bunch of boys that live here and they do some weird things in the forest."

Just then the worn path disappeared into a large open area of the forest where the trees had obviously been cut down and bushes cleared. The sun was able to pierce through a hole in an area void of trees. It was then that I noticed neat rows of plants planted in a manner very similar to corn rows. The plants were about four feet tall and had large, funny fanned leaves coming out of the stocks. There must have been over 100 plants growing neatly in the rows. The furrows next to the plants was wet and obviously had been recently watered.

"The Dark boys must like gardening," I remarked.

By now Dwayne was walking even slower and in a hunched position down the rows of plants.

"What…? "

"Shhhhh!" Dwayne exclaimed, turning back toward me with his right pointing finger over his lips. "Can you whisper, you idiot? Do you want them to hear us?"

I nodded my head up and down and slowly put my right finger over my lips to signify that I would be quiet. What was the big deal, I thought. I loved to garden. Mom and I had a beautiful garden and I would love to talk gardening with these Dark boys.

Linda was standing behind me, not saying a thing. She obviously knew not to talk unless asked to. It was while looking back at her that I noticed again that she was pretty cute. Her dark brown hair and light eyes really intrigued me. She would always give me a half-cocked smile that showed her cute dimples.

"What kind of plants are these?" I whispered to Dwayne.

"I don't know, but I know they don't like people walking through them. They yelled at me and chased me last year when I walked through the plants. Of course, the plants were a lot taller then and they could not see where I was going."

Just as we exited the neatly hoed furrow, the worn path began again turning east back toward the Steinboton property.

"Bear," I whispered.

Both Bear and Rusty were having fun running through the plants, attacking each other in fun play. Both dogs were at least sixty pounds each and their rough play was breaking the stocks of the nice plants. It seemed someone could probably hear the snapping of the plants from far away. Bear was not listening to me because she was having so much fun. I turned around and walked back toward the dogs. Within a matter of seconds I was upon them, just in time for them to run from me, knocking down ten or twelve more plants. It was obvious that they thought that I was playing a game with them. Dwayne was not amused and soon was by my side trying to round up the dogs. The more we tried the more intently the dogs were determined to play and run around the Dark garden, knocking down plants. It was obvious by then that we had no control over the dogs playing and decided to just leave them, hoping that they would soon follow.

The three of us resumed our hike out of the plants onto the trail back into the forest. We paid no attention to the dogs or their whereabouts. After walking about another 200 feet, Dwayne stopped and turned back to us and raised his hand and arm in one motion, with his hand straight out telling us to stop.

Dwayne turned to his left and pointed to a large maple tree. "There it is," he said, while pointing his finger toward the tree.

I glanced toward the tree and noticed a silver box about the size of a small ice chest. Upon closer observation, I noticed it was made of galvanized steel and sat up against the tree, slightly tilting to the left due to the uneven ground upon which it sat. There was a large latch that folded over the top to the side of the box where a lock would fit. As Dwayne bent down to pick up the box, I noticed that no lock was on it. Dwayne walked over behind the tree and carefully set the box down.

Dwayne looked up, waiving his left arm in a slicing motion. "Linda wait there; Fred come over here," Dwayne exclaimed with excitement.

Linda complied and took the last step in her stride just a few feet from the tree. She sat down on the leaf filled ground, Indian style. As I approached the back of the tree, Dwayne already had the box top open and was pulling out magazines and weird looking pipes that were made of beautiful glass.

"What are those pipes for?"

"I don't know but they look really cool."

I was about ready to grab a magazine that Dwayne had set on the ground front side down when I heard a gun shot and a shout.

"Get out of here!" someone yelled in a very gruff voice. The sound was coming from the clearing area. Another gunshot rang out. It was clearly a small caliber gun because it did not sound too loud. It sounded like a twenty-two rifle. Just then the dogs rounded the trail and headed straight toward us.

Dwayne and I looked up and very briefly looked at each other. We did not have to say anything. Dwayne's eyes said everything. He dropped the pipes from his right hand and began to run down the path farther away from the opening. Linda must have gotten up fast because before I took my first step, she was in a full run passing to my right.

At that point I heard the huffing and puffing of a person coming down the path. I started to run like I had never run before in my life. I did not look back as I began to distance myself from the heavy breathing. I heard a few shots and bullets striking the branches next to me. There was light ahead and I could see Grandpa and Grandma Davis's chicken coop—safety was within reach.

CHAPTER FOURTEEN
THE DARK BOYS

Dwayne, Linda and I walked through the Davis pasture toward the road, each of us now breathing a little bit easier. The pasture was slightly wet and the lush green heavily grazed grass was easy to walk on. Linda was close to my left and Dwayne was slightly ahead of me to the right.

"Look," Dwayne said, pointing his finger toward the road.

I looked and saw a number of kids playing what looked like baseball across the Davis field next to the entrance to the main dirt road.

"Hey, I don't remember them telling us anything about a baseball game," I exclaimed.

"Who cares," Dwayne uttered, "Let's go play."

Dwayne's walk soon became a trot. Linda did not break her stride but kept walking, looking down at the occasional dandelion flower in the pasture. I instinctively started to follow Dwayne, but then

210

after a quick thought decided to take my time and hang back with Linda.

"So were you scared back there in the Dark's forest?" I asked, turning to my right toward .

She was still walking but looking down and occasionally to the right, clearly trying to avoid my eyes. "No, Dwayne and I always sneak back there. I think it is exciting to see if the Dark boys will ever catch us."

"How many Darks are there?

Linda now turned to look me in the eye only for a second before she moved her gaze to the grass. "Oh, the mom and dad and three or four boys. They all have long hair and hang out at their house a lot."

"Why?"

"I don't know. We can just hear them at times in the forest doing something with machines or making loud noises, you know something like work. Ah, I don't know. Why are you asking so many questions?"

I paused while taking another step or two. "I don't know. I was just curious."

Linda gazed at me again with a slight smile. "You know what they say—curiosity always kills the cat."

That smirkey smile just killed me; she looked so cute and innocent with her smile, but I knew better. She was the mischievous type that loved to hang out with the boys and do everything that her brother did.

We walked for another minute or two, side by side until we reached the gate in the pasture that lead us over a dirt road and into the other pasture where the other kids were playing ball. The noise was getting louder and Dwayne was some thirty feet in front of us now, already near the make-shift home plate.

I was not interested in any baseball now, but just wanted to keep walking and talking with Linda. I opened the gate that was made of old rusted round pipe, allowed Linda to step through, then latched it behind me. This was the only gate I had seen since we moved to Penryn that actually had a latch. I bent down and picked up a small circular shaped rock off the road and threw it at a post. A direct hit.

"Nice shot Fred," Linda said while she bent down to pick up a similar rock for herself.

"Let's see if I can hit the post also." She wound up like a professional pitcher and with all of her might threw the rock. "Bang," the rock hit dead on, right in the middle of the six by six inch post.

"Wow, what a throw! Where did you learn to throw like that?"

"Plum fights."

"Huh, what do you mean?" I asked in a curious voice.

"Well, you see, Dwayne and I always play plum fights where we each have a tree as a base and try and hit each other with plums. It's fun." She grimily smiled and looked up at me. "But it ruins our clothes."

"You mean Dwayne has experience in plum fights?"

"Years of experience and he never loses to any neighbor kid."

I nodded and thought to myself, I've got it now. Dwayne always acts dumb but really is smarter than all of us. He puts us off guard and then swoops in for the attack no matter what he is doing. I bet he knew exactly what he was doing when we went into the Dark forest. Out of my daydream, I was back looking at Linda walking slightly in front of me.

"Come on you guys. Hurry up and we will let you play," yelled one of the boys from the pasture. It was a lower teenage voice, which I had not heard before.

As Linda and I approached, we saw a group of neighbor kids standing in the field around a make-shift baseball diamond. The pitching mound was about eight inches high, with a small, flat, old grey two by four inch board pushed halfway into the top of the make-shift pitchers mound. One side of the mound was worn away so that if the pitcher was to step off the edge of the board he would twist his ankle. The board was grey with age and one could see it had a few nails still in it clearly used to help anchor the board into the dirt.

"Hey batter, batter, batter," the chatter sounded as we neared. Scott was up to bat and Stewart was pitching. The ball was an old partially ripped brown baseball that had looked like the dog had been chewing on. No doubt this was one of our baseballs that Bear had played with many times.

Stewart wound up and threw the ball toward Scott. Scott spun quickly on his heel to his left to avoid the poorly thrown pitch.

"Ouch!" Scott yelled as the ball struck him on the right arm. I could hear the loud thump even from where I was standing, which was many feet from the plate. Scott slumped over and then sat on the dirt still holding the bat in his right hand. He reached over, grabbed a rock and threw it at Stewart while still in the seated position, but the rock made it only halfway to Stewart.

"Thanks Tooth; I think you broke my arm." Scott was holding his arm and rocking back and forth in the seated position and soon everyone had gathered around him.

"Are you okay?" everyone was asking.

Stewart was still standing on the mound, smart enough to stay away from Scott so that he was out of reach just in case Scott went on one of his tyrant rages.

That was the end of the game. Usually it took a more serious injury to stop a game, but no one seemed interested in playing baseball anymore. As I stood with the rest of the kids in the circle, I noticed a dark haired boy and girl that I had not seen before. I was directly across the circle of people from the girl. She was tall with jet black straight hair that came to the middle of her back. She had piercing dark eyes with her skin slightly tan in color. She looked about eighteen, though; she was probably no more than thirteen or fourteen years old. She had a perfectly shaped body and was fully developed unlike all the other girls our age. She caught me staring intently at her and cracked a slight smile as if to say, are you enjoying what you see? Yes, I thought, and the white tank top she was wearing was not helping much.

A few seconds after I realized that I was caught staring at her, I quickly looked away to avoid her eyes. The other boy was obviously her younger brother whose face was a spitting image of her but obviously the boy version. His hair was long, about down to his shoulders, but wavy on the top with large bouncing curls. Clearly this was competition for us boys as the girls would be falling all over him. He had piercing blue eyes that caught your attention. I looked at him and nodded my head up and down, acknowledging his presence. He nodded back and then turned and started to walk away.

"Why are you leaving?" Stewart asked, still standing on the pitchers mound.

"Aw, got to get home," the boy said.

"Hey what is your name?" I yelled.

He did not stop but just turned his head while continuing to walk. "Steve Smith."

I motioned with my arm and right index finger toward the beautiful dark-haired girl: "What's your name?"

Already walking with her brother, she turned her head toward me without breaking stride with her brother and said, "Lynn." She said it in a sexy way and cracked a slight smile, then whipped her head back around causing her shiny jet black hair to flip around like a model you would see on television.

Just then I caught something out of the corner of my eye. It was three people walking down the dirt road that passed near out houses. They were coming toward the few of us that were left still looking at Scott on the ground in the make-shift baseball field. My attention was off of Linda and now on the figures that were coming closer to our field. I could see that it was what looked like three boys, all of whom were about the same size but looked exceptionally large in stature. One boy had short brown hair while the other two boys had long shoulder length hair, one brown and one blonde.

"Ooops," Dwayne gulped.

"What?" I asked

Dwayne was now standing right next to me looking at the boys. Scott was now just now getting up and only a few feet from my back.

Dwayne cleared his throat and gulped, "That's the Dark boys."

Dwayne looked visibly scared and turned back around so as to not face the boys. He slowly started to walk toward the bat that was lying next to the home plate that Scott had dropped. Dwayne grabbed the bat in his right hand and placed it over his right shoulder. It was then that I got the hint. There was a large fist sized, almost perfectly round rock only a few feet from my feet. I slowly stretched my right leg and foot out toward the rock and with my shoe pulled it over right next to me on the ground. However, I thought that if anything happened, there was no sized rock that would do anything to those three boys that were twice our size. I made a quick survey and realized that everyone else had just quietly started to walk away. It was only Dwayne, Stewart, a weak kneed Scott, and I standing there when the boys finally approached.

One of the long haired guys stepped slightly forward of the other two. "What's up guys?" He was clearly the youngest but seemed to be the one that was going to do all the talking.

Dwayne reached his left arm up, palm out. "Hi, Willie. What's going on?"

The blonde haired boy just stared at him and did not reply, then said "Someone has been on our property and messing with some of our equipment and…" The stocky blonde boy paused and narrowed his eyes.

"Our vegetable garden," the other tall and stocky clean-cut boy said.

Scott and Stewart obviously looked puzzled. Stewart snickered and shook his head as if to say, "What are you talking about?" I knew that Stewart had a smart mouth from the short time I knew him, and I was worried that his mouth would get us in trouble.

The long and brown haired boy turned his head away from Dwayne and me toward Stewart. The look on his face was obviously one of displeasure. This guy looked like he was at least a junior or senior in high school. His lips tightened and he put his left hand to his lip. "Some of you guys are new around here, aren't you?"

No one knew what to say so we all just stood there, not saying a word. Dwayne was now clearly nervous, looking down at the ground and swirling his foot into the dirt in a attempt to make some sort of pattern.

Stewart piped up, "Yeah and…." Stewart paused.

"Well I don't know who it was but if we catch any of you on our property messing with our stuff, all three of us will kick your butts."

"You'll kick my what?" Stewart said in a smart feisty tone.

The long and brown haired boy chuckled and took two steps toward Stewart. Stewart did not move but started to stare him down. Of course Stewart was not looking down but straight up at the much bigger boy.

"You have quite a smart mouth for a short little boy that has a momma that dresses him in weird mutli-colored pants."

Stewart was wearing one of his signature pants, an old pair of Levi bell-bottoms with upside down back pockets and blue corduroy material sewn on the bottom portion of his pants near the cuff to repair an area that has been previously worn and torn.

There was silence and then Stewart reared his right leg back and forth and kicked the dust and rocks under his foot toward the boy causing rocks, dirt and dust to strike the boys clean jeans. Stewart was clearly not backing down.

I took another scan of the area and realized that all our supposed friends were now gone. It was us four younger boys against three older and bigger boys. The odds did not look good; however I had a rock at my disposal and Dwayne had a thirty-two inch Easton wood bat. I wondered, though, if Dwayne had the guts to use the bat if needed or if he would drop it and run away.

The blonde boy nodded his head up and down and turned toward Stewart. "Look, little man, we can hurt you and your friends real bad if we wanted to, so just give us the names of those who were on our property messing with our…" he paused, "vegetable garden, and no one will go home crying with a broken arm or leg." The blonde boy was now hitting his right fist into his open left hand.

Stewart popped off again. "Yeah, it's gonna suck when your parents have to run you guys to the hospital to fix your broken arms and legs."

Just then, the roar of a truck was heard coming down the dirt road. I could see a billow of dust headed our way and what looked like Grandpa Davis's yellow Toyota Helux truck. Sure enough, within a matter of seconds the pick-up came to a stop on the dirt road some fifty feet from where we were all standing by the side of the road.

Grandpa Davis was a large man with wispy white hair on the back of his head and a little bit on the side as well. He wore old-style wire rimmed glasses. He was about six feet two inches tall and was as square as a block. I know he weighed at least 235 lbs because he would always complain about not being able to lose enough weight to get down to his desired weight of 230 lbs. The Dark boys could see that his arms, like Popeye's arms, were extremely large in the bicep area.

When grandpa got out of his truck and started to walk toward us, the boys' demeanor changed. His walk was more of a waddle as grandpa was run over by a semi truck as a young man and never healed properly from the accident.

The blonde boy leaned toward us as Grandpa approached, with narrowed eyes and a sneering expression on his lips. "You're lucky your grandpa saved y…."

"You mean saved you from taking a long trip to the hospital?" Stewart interrupted, chuckling.

Before grandpa reached us the three boys turned and started to walk away.

"Hey, young men, come here." Grandpa gestured with his right arm. The boys stopped as grandpa turned from us and walked toward them. We could hear the conversation as grandpa approached.

"Say fellas, you wouldn't be the Dark boys?

"Why, yes we are," answered the blonde boy. "I'm Willie, this is Woody and that is Steve."

"A pleasure to meet you. I am your new neighbor and it would be a pleasure to meet your parents some day."

Willie's eyes started to narrow toward me as he looked around grandpa's wide body. I turned to my right and looked at Stewart who was holding up his right hand with the middle index finger straight up. I reached over and slapped his hand down.

"Knock it off Stewart; don't you know when to stop? You're going to get us killed!"

"No, I'll break their necks just like I do to the rabbits."

CHAPTER FIFTEEN
UNCLE ART

Uncle Art and Aunt Jackie walked in through the garage door. "Hello, knock, knock!" exclaimed Uncle Art. Uncle Art was an elderly, tall, slender man standing about six feet three inches. His round pudgy face and large deep-set eyes did not seem to match his thin frame. His unmistaken smile was always as wide as a bus and was his signature expression. His lips were large with the lower lip always hanging down a few inches from his short stubby chin. He had large soft hands from his years of working behind a desk as an insurance salesman. Uncle Art always had to be right and would rarely back down from his opinion. As kids we loved to see him and Grandma Davis get together because they would always argue over the littlest things.

Aunt Jackie was grandma Davis's sister. She was a spry, short, red-headed elderly woman that always had spunk in her walk. She was wearing a light green summer dress with large flowers all over the fabric, almost to the point of covering up the underlying green color of the dress. Her one partially gold tooth always showed when she smiled. She always was happy, never saying, at least outwardly, anything negative about anyone or anything. She would always tell me that the glass was half full, not half empty.

"Come in," Dad yelled from the living room.

"Hello Fred." Art approached my dad who was sitting on the red and yellow flowered couch watching local news.

Sticking out his hand toward Dad, Art bent down slightly to look into his eyes.

"What are you watching?"

"Oh nothing but the same old thing: murder in Sacramento, the President back peddling and the liberal Democrats screwing things up.

Dad was extremely conservative when it came to politics. He registered as a Democrat so that he could vote in the primary election for the person that he thought could not beat a Republican.

Auntie Jackie put out her arms. "Hello Fred," "Hi Jackie" They embraced, but you could see Dad was not enjoying it.

"Where is everyone?" Jackie asked. It was obvious everyone was in the kitchen, as the clanking from the dinner preparation could be heard from the maroon-carpeted living room.

Jackie turned to her left and walked down the long, red, linoleum-lined hall toward Mom and me who were in the kitchen. Mom was preparing a chuck roast in her old-black iron kettle and I was sitting on the old, grey covered bar stool drinking an A&W root beer. The chuck roast filled the kitchen with the sweet smell of Mom's great cooking.

"Hi Annie, how are you doing?" Jackie asked.

"Fine."

Grandma Davis came around the corner from the sunken living room where she was with Scott, playing some sort of card game, something that Grandma loved to do every time she came over to the house.

"Why, hello. Hello my little sister."

"Hello, hello!" Jackie exclaimed.

Grandma turned to Mom. "Is there anything Jackie and I can do to help, Anne?"

"No, dinner is just about ready. Why don't you gather everyone up to the table."

Mom was using an old wooden handled potato masher to mash up the potatoes. The thick, brown gravy was boiling in the old iron skillet that Mom had cooked the roast in. I couldn't wait to eat the roast that would tear apart with the pull of a fork.

"Come and eat," Mom yelled after Grandma couldn't get anyone to come to the table.

Soon everyone began to migrate toward the small circular table that was crowded with seven chairs around it. The large window in the dining area next to the table made the dinner atmosphere even more enjoyable. The beautiful large plum trees that lined the large, deep, green back lawn were visible from the open window. Scott and I scooted past the tightly placed chairs to the back side of the table next to the window. This gave the older people easier access to their chairs. Grandpa and Grandma Davis made their way and sat down closest to the bathroom wall which butted up against the dining room. Dad and Mom sat in their usual spots, Dad closest to the bar which separated the kitchen from the dining room and Mom's seat closet to the kitchen so that she could get up and down as needed. Art and Jackie sat next to the Grandma and Grandpa.

"Art would you like to say the blessing on the food?" Father asked. Mom's eyes rolled and I could hear Scott sigh quietly under his breath, knowing that the prayer would be long.

"I would love to. Dear Heavenly Father, we gather ourselves together today in this beautiful home and at this beautiful time of year. We thank thee for the beautiful land in which we live, the beautiful farm that Fred and Anne have invited us to enjoy…."

I sat there with my arms folded and right eye slightly open looking around the table. Mom would turn her head every few seconds to look at the corn still boiling on the stove. You see, Uncle Art is well known for his long, drawn out prayers.

"And Lord, we thank thee for this fine meal of meat, potatoes…" Uncle Art paused, "and, and other things that Anne has fixed. We bless that this food will nourish and strengthen our bodies so that we may be able to go forth and do thy work here on the earth. May we…."

I could now see Aunt Jackie starting to open the left corner of her eye looking at Art. Frustrated, Dad had reached over and quietly grabbed a roll and put it on his plate and was slowly spreading butter over the top. Just as I turned back, Aunt Jackie's left elbow, arms still folded position, jabbed Uncle Art in the rubs. Uncle Art did not flinch.

"And dear Lord as we again close with another supplication to thee, bless all the missionaries in the field...."

With one arm still folded, Scott and I, at almost the same time, reached our right hand into the bowl filled with hot rolls. We each grabbed one and quietly and very carefully cut open and buttered our roll. Mom still had her hands folded and eyes shut along with Grandpa Davis. Grandma had her eyes open by this time and was smiling at us boys for taking a roll. Grandpa was obviously enjoying this prayer because it was always a family joke to see who would give the longest prayers, Grandpa Davis or Uncle Art. One time Dad actually got the good old super-eight video camera out and took a video of Uncle Art saying a prayer. He almost ran out of film.

"...So Lord, bless this food and this family again with your good grace in the name of...."

"Amen," Amen," Amen," everyone said in almost perfect unity, interrupting Uncle Art from finishing the last part of the prayer.

Scott and I had to sit there for just a minute because Dad's rules were clear—adults dish up first and then kids. I hated this as Grandpa was always very slow in dishing up his plate.

Finally, Scott and I were able to dish up some of Mom's roast and mashed potatoes and gravy.

"So when does school start, boys?" Grandpa Floyd asked while chewing on a piece of roast.

I answered, "Next week, I think."

"You think but you don't know?"

Grandma Davis interrupted. "Now leave those boys alone Floyd; they don't care about that."

"Listen Myrna!" Grandpa Davis always called Grandma "Myrna" when he was getting mad and "Babe" when he wanted something. Grandpa raised his right index finger and paused as if starting to talk but lowered his finger and just continued to look down and eat his steaming hot dinner. Grandpa knew who was in charge— not him.

There was no talking for a good two or three minutes as everyone was too busy enjoying the delicious meal of chuck roast, mashed potatoes and gravy, hot homemade rolls, fresh corn and butter laden squash from our garden. The peaceful silence was interrupted.

"Excuse me for a minute; I need to use the little boy's room."

Uncle Art pulled his napkin from the neck of his shirt and placed it carefully on the right side of his half plate of food. Taking both of his arms he pushed the old wooden table chair behind him, stood up and turned to his right toward the bathroom. He did not have to take more than about four or five steps to reach the bathroom door. I heard the door open and shut and then heard the distinctive clank of the toilet seat dropping onto the toilet bowl.

"Mmmm, this corn is out of this world," Grandpa stated with his mouth half full of corn.

I could hear the popping of corn around the table. The Nickel and Davis families always ate their corn like typing on an old typewriter. We would eat it in a row, biting hard down on the corn in even rows, turning it once we reached the end, then making our way back to the other side of the row. Grandpa now had at least five or six cornels of buttery corn stuck to his chin.

The sound of every one eating their corn was suddenly interrupted with the loud echoing sound of Uncle Art passing gas while going to the bathroom. I could see my father directly across from me. He was in the middle of taking another bite of corn when he stopped with the ear of corn still in his mouth. He raised his eyebrows and slowly put the corn down. Grandpa Davis was sitting next to Dad and was in the process of placing a large portion of potatoes and gravy into his mouth. He stopped, shrugged his shoulders and tightened his lips as if to say "Oh well" and continued to eat. Uncle Art then repeated with low grunts and loud farts, sometimes three or four farts right in a row followed by a long loud sigh of relief. By this time Aunt Jackie and Grandma Davis were laughing under their breath, and Grandma's eyes welling up with tears due to her attempt to stop from laughing out loud. I could not hold it much longer—if I heard one more fart and sigh of relief I would not be able to hold my laughter. I remembered back when Dad was having our house built. He had to figure out a way to save money so he did not put any insulation in the interior walls. This was now playing out to be a mistake, having the bathroom so close to the kitchen dining area without insulation in the bathroom walls.

Just as I thought it would end, there were another loud five or six rapid fire of farts in a row. That was it.

"Blaaa, ha ha ha!" Scott broke out laughing out loud, spewing potatoes and gravy out of his mouth all over the table. Without looking at anyone else I bowed my head down with my chin touching the top of my chest and began to chuckle out loud, trying so hard to not laugh snot began to run out of my nose. Then everyone started to laugh, Jackie slapping the table with her right hand as her body shook with her loud laughter. Dad just waved his hand in front of his nose back and forth as if to indicate that something did not smell well. Grandpa on the other hand paid no mind to what was going on because this is something that he probably did himself many times. He just kept laughing and eating his dinner.

After what seemed like an eternity but was only about ten minutes, we heard the toilet flush. The walls were so thin that you could hear that water run through them after the flush. However, it was obvious that the water was not flowing very well. By now no one was eating except Grandpa Davis and everyone was just looking at each other smiling and snickering. Everyone sat there to wait to hear what was next. Sure enough I could hear the sound of a plunger being used on the toilet and could just barely make out Uncle Art talking to himself.

"Damn toilet! Get down there! Come-on you bugger, get down there!" I could hear the sloshing of water and finally the water passing through the pipes under the raised wood floor. Art wrestled a little more in the bathroom before I heard the distinctive click of the knob being unlocked from the bath room. The squeaky door creaked open and I could hear Uncle Art walking out of the door. I thought to myself, "Did he wash his hands?" I didn't remember hearing the faucet run in the bath room. "Oh gross," I thought. I took a quick glance around the table and Scott had three or four napkins full of food that he was cleaning off of the table. Dad had a mean scowl on his face clearly from Scott ruining the food by plastering all the uneaten food. Jackie, Mom and Grandma Davis were all red in the face and were all wiping the tears from their eyes from laughing so hard. Art came out of the bathroom door and took about six steps, briefly looked around the table, pulled his chair back a little farther than it was with his left hand, lifted his left foot around the front of the chair and sat down. There was no expression on his face other than the typical movement of his lower lip over his top lip. He slid his chair up to the table, grabbed his napkin, then tucked it between his neck and shirt, paused, and looked up.

"Annie, can you please pass me some more potatoes?"

Chapter Sixteen
Getting Shot At!

The next morning I was on the phone to all the Penyrn boys. My first call was to Owen. I heard three rings in the headset, then….

"Hello, the Hawk trailer."

"What's up Owen?"

"Hey Fred." A short pause ensued.

"What you got going?"

"Just watching some Saturday morning cartoons."

"Which ones?"

"The Road Runner and Bugs Bunny." Owen paused and then perked up a little more. "Do you want to do something?"

"Sure, what?"

"I don't know." Owen stated in a frustrated tone of voice like he was being bothered.

"Well, school starts in a few days and I want to try and find the Bickford cave again," I said.

"I don't know where it is." Owen's voice now changed to one of curiosity and interest.

"Neither do I," I said.

"Call Dwayne and then call me back."

I began calling each one of the Penryn boys and it seemed everyone had the same thing on their mind, to make one last trip to find Bickford Ranch before school started on Monday. I asked Dwayne if he could bring his sister with him and he laughed.

"What are you laughing at?"

"Well, I will ask my dad if it's okay if Linda goes with me to the caves so that she can see…."

"No," I interrupted." Don't tell your dad anything. He will shoot me the next time I come over.

"Okay, I'll ask Linda. I will see you in a few minutes."

Soon, Tooth, Dwayne, (no Linda this time), Stewart, Ron, Scott, and I were standing outside our front door on the porch preparing to take the dangerous walk across the Shepman field to Owen's house.

Everyone stood up and began to walk down the old, used greasy rail-road stairs that were in front of our house. Stewart sat on the porch and did not move.

"Hey, let's go," Scott called out to Stewart.

"Wait a minute guys. I have an idea." Stewart replied.

We all stopped at the bottom of the stairs and each turned back toward Stewart. I set my Crossman BB gun down on the freshly cut grass. Stewart continued.

"Let's take some inner tubes and float down the canal to Bickford Ranch. Remember, I heard some of the local kids do that and that the ditch can get going real fast."

Scott shrugged his shoulders, tightened his lips, narrowed his eyes and started to slowly bob his head up and down. By now each of us were looking at Scott for direction and it was clear from the expression on his face that he approved of the idea. Scott set down his gun down next to mine and started to walk down the grass area toward the garage. We all just stood there and watched as he turned the corner into the garage.

Within a matter of a minute Scott came back around the corner from the garage with what looked like three or four flat car-tire inner tubes slung through his arms and onto his right shoulder. Stewart stood up.

"There you go; that is what I am talking about."

"But what about our BB guns?" Dwayne asked in a cracking voice.

Scott approached Dwayne without a change of expression.

"I guess you better make sure that you don't fall off your tube and get that gun wet." Scott paused. Or, do you want to go into Bickford forest without a BB gun?"

Dwayne's voice stated to crack even more: "No."

"Then let's get going. Owen has a pump at his house and we can pump these things up. I know he also has some more inner tubes that we can use."

Scott leaned over and stretched forth his left arm to pick up his BB gun. I followed suit and soon we were pounding through the weeds down the south-side hill on our property towards Mr. Shepman's property. Bear and Zeke were following us as usual and that made me feel good, that we had two big dogs with us to protect us from wild animals when we reached Bickford Ranch.

It was no more than a minute when we reached the old barbed wire fence that separated our ranch from the Shepman's. Again, there was no other way to get to Owens's house than to cross Shepman's pasture. To go around the ranch would require asking Mom for a ride and an explanation what were going to do over at Owen's. We learned at an early age not to lie and we took that seriously because if Dad ever caught us in a lie, we would be severely beaten on the butt with the long gnarled bamboo stick. However, we learned that we did not have to lie if we just did not tell Mom everything that we were doing. We just told her that we were going to go shooting around the property and maybe over to Owen's house for awhile. She never asked the important, smart question of what else we were going to do. Mom lived a very sheltered life and was trusting and had no idea what we were doing half the time. Now Dad, he was very wise to the world and I believe he had a good idea of some of the things that we might be doing during the day while he was at work. Dad was out of his house when he was fifteen years old and had to fend for himself until he lied about his age and was able to get into the United States Marine Corps at seventeen. We could not pull the wool over his eyes.

"Well, does anyone see old Shepman?" Scott asked as he turned his head back and forth to look at each of us.

Stewart was standing next to the fence with his BB gun in his right hand and his left hand on the top piece of the old rusty barbed wire. "Nope, I don't see or hear anything, I don't even hear his sheep."

There was nothing in the pasture: no sheep, no cows or bulls. Shepman had to be around somewhere as he never left the property. In fact, the rumor was that he did not even leave to get groceries. He would have his younger sister go to the store and shop for his groceries. He didn't need anything else as he had enough junk around the old trailer to fix anything that might break.

I squinted and tried to take a closer look up on top of the hill near his trailer. I could see his tan-colored 1964 square bed Ford pick-up that was still sitting in the dirt driveway. But he rarely left the property, and that thing was always sitting in front of his trailer, I thought.

Stewart lifted up the middle two barbed wires, put his right and then left leg through and stepped onto the lush green property of Mr. Shepman. Soon everyone followed suit and the next thing you know boys and dogs were frolicking around the Shepman property.

"Wow, it's kind of nice to not have cows chasing us or Shepman shooting at us," Ron said as he walked proudly in his Levi cut-off shorts.

It was an enjoyable walk across the lush irrigated pasture. There were no worries, no cows, bulls, or Mr. Shepman to deal with. I stopped along with the other boys at the base of the large oak-covered hill to step into the cool refreshing Clover Valley Creek. It was only a matter of seconds before we all had our shoes and socks off and were walking in the cool foothill creek. The water was no deeper than to our calves, but it felt good in the late-August heat. There was a slight breeze that cooled down the effects of the hot sun and the cool water that penetrated our now bare feet. It felt like the breeze brought our body temperatures down a few degrees.

Stewart and I sat on the large, old oak tree stump that was next to the water to put on our socks and shoes. All the other boys were still kicking the water on each other, and Bear and Zeke were running up and down the creek chasing after each other. After a few minutes the other boys stopped and sat down on the large rotting oak log that crossed the stream and dressed to get ready to leave. Stewart and I patiently waited for the other boys to finish and sat and enjoyed the cool late summer breeze. It was then that I first noticed something new on Stewart. He had a Levi jeans back pocket that had been cut in half and sewn together to make a smaller Levi jeans rear pocket that had been sewn onto the front pocket of his vertical striped t-shirt.

"You guys ready?" Scott asked, bending over and using his arms to push himself up so as to stand on the old rotting log. He wobbled a little, putting his left and right arms out like wings to balance himself.

"Sure, sure, yeah," everyone replied.

From the creek it was a straight uphill climb through the oak trees to the top of the hill where we would be able to first see Owen's house. Stewart and Scott were walking fast, stretching their legs as far as they could to take bigger steps to speed up their ascent to the top. We could not keep up with their long steps, but we were still no more than a few feet behind them as they crested the top of the slope and then headed down the back side of the hill. From the top, I could see at the bottom of the hill a large pond and I could also see the Clover Valley stream that emptied into it. Of course, when Bear and Zeke saw the pond they immediately made a beeline for the water. Bear was in front and Zeke was close behind. I turned away, following the guys toward Owen's house when I heard the loud splashing sound of Bear and Zeke hitting the water. They never just walked into the water; they would always take a flying leap into the water landing with like a human belly flop.

Now, lagging behind no more than just a foot or two from the boys, I noticed something behind a tree next to the pond. I stopped.

"Hey guys," I whispered. "Stop guys, stop, hold on," I said, raising my left hand into the air toward them. I continued in a whispered voice.

"Something is over by the pond and I think it's a deer." Stewart turned and took a few steps back, and, with me, peered at the pond. However, the rest of the boys continued to walk towards Owen's house, not stopping to see what I had thought I encountered. After a few second pause I saw old rancher Shepman coming out from behind the tree, zipping up his pants, obviously finishing up taking a pee. With his back still toward us and his eyes fixed on the dogs swimming in the pond, he reached with his left arm toward the tree where he grabbed a small rifle. It looked like a 22 rifle, probably the same one he used to shoot at kids when they crossed his property. Stewart and I were standing still near a few small oak trees and blended in enough so that the old man could not see us yet. I turned my head toward Stewart and he raised his right index finger to his lips to quiet me. The other boys had almost reached the next very small hill and were almost out of sight. There were enough oak trees that Shepman could not see them. However, Stewart and I were no more than fifty yards away from him, and all he really had to do was turn around and he would probably see us. We did not move but watched him eye our dogs again.

Bear and Zeke were almost to the other side of the pond getting ready to get out when I saw Shepman raise his 22, left arm holding the barrel, and the stock held firmly against his right shoulder.

"Bear, here!" I shouted and blew two quick whistles.

At that instant Stewart began to run full speed toward the next small hill and toward Owen's house, weaving in and out of the small and medium sized valley and heritage oak trees.

"Pop, Pop, Pop!"

Shepman was now shooting, but at who or what I was not sure. There were no sounds of breaking branches near us. It was rumored that Shepman was a veteran of the Vietnam War and ever since he got home he had became a recluse and was very weird. At that second what worried me was that he might be a crack shot with a rifle. I know neighbors had complained that one of their dogs had been found dead with a 22 bullet hole in its head.

"Pop, Pop!" Now the branches around us were making a snapping noise and I could hear the whistle of something passing to the left of us. It was obviously a bullet. At that time I had a weird feeling, like a state of being in shock. I could not hear anything but my heart and head thumping, and all over noises sounded muffled. My focus was to get out of there alive. I looked back and could see Bear and Zeke running full bore toward us.

What seemed like an eternity probably only lasted a few seconds. Steve and I finally crested and went down the other side of the small hill. Bear and Zeke were now at least twenty or thirty feet in front us of. My run now became an easy trot, allowing Stewart to catch up. As we reached safety, I stopped, bent over and placed both of my hands on my upper thighs.

Huffing and puffing I asked, "Stewart, did we lose him?"

"Yeah, I think so."

"Let's not stop, but at least start walking," I was barely able to gasp out. I knew old man

Shepman could not walk very fast and I figured we were out of harms way. After walking down the hill we could see the fence that separated Shepman's ranch and Owen's house. I could see, in the distance, Owen and the other guys standing in the back yard talking.

Standing next to me, Stewart reached over with his left arm and patted my back. "Lets pick it up. I don't want to get caught on the wrong side of the fence if Shepman decides to try to make it up over the hill."

Chapter Seventeen
Bickford Ranch Mine

Stewart kicked a small rock that was in front of him on Clark Tunnel Road. All six Penryn boys were walking side by side taking up most of the patched, chuckhole filled old Clark Tunnel Road. We had decided to leave the inner tubes behind at Owen's house, realizing we could only float back down toward the valley with them. We would definitely do that another day. Today we would explore Bickford Ranch! Only Steve, Dwayne and I had our BB guns with us and both Zeke and Bear were off in the weeds along the road, sniffing out everything. The early afternoon sun was bright, but the cool Delta breeze was still blowing. We had just left Owen's dirt driveway that dumped out onto Clark Tunnel Road. We had a long walk ahead of us to make it to the area where the Bickford caves were, by legend, supposed to be. The properties that lined the old cracked paved road were beautiful, with only a few houses and beautiful peach, plum and mandarin orchards on both sides of the road. After ten or fifteen minutes walking on the road, with not even one car passing, we reached a large carved-out mountain tunnel that had the road running right through it. Large water pipes crossed overhead that were sagging just slightly with the weight of the water in the old rusted iron pipes. The Piltz farm was on the left, lined with beautiful green mandarin and peach trees. There were a number of peach trees that were loaded with yellow and white large peaches. It was tempting to walk over and grab a peach and I knew the Piltz family would probably not mind.

"Anyone hungry for a peach?" I asked.

"No" everyone replied. So I didn't have one, either. Bear and Zeke were running through the knee-high grass that was under each one of the peach trees. Scott shouted, "Bear, come on," waving his left arm back toward his body. The road curved to the right and then the left where the gated railroad dirt road went off to the right and up toward the tracks. This was one of our routes to the tracks from Owens's house. We could more easily access Bickford from the tracks but we would have to make a dangerous run through the long, dark and narrow Clark train tunnel. That wasn't an option: We didn't need to even ask each other. Everyone knew to just keep walking up the hill until we reached the summit of Clark Tunnel Road. At the summit the road turned into a rut filled compacted dirt road. The sound of the small dirt granite pebbles on the road being stepped on made a distinct sound similar to someone using course sandpaper on wood. The dust billowed up behind us as we walked on the decomposed granite road.

"Pop, pop, pop, dang it!" Stewart exclaimed as he lowered his BB gun away from the area where he was aiming at a small sparrow.

"What did you think you were going to hit? That little bird?" I asked.

"Of course," Stewart snapped, shaking his head in dismay.

"Have you killed one yet?" I asked.

Stewart kept walking, now with the Daisy BB gun hanging on the right side of his hip. "Well, ah, no, but I have almost hit a few."

"Good, I now feel better that you are here to protect us with your BB gun."

"Shut up Fred. Let's see you do it."

"No, I'm not stupid enough to try and hit a little flying bird with a BB gun."

I could see a billow of dust in the distance from what was obviously a car traveling quite fast down the old dusty road.

"Car!" someone yelled.

Zeke and Bear were not around us. They were both in the fields, smelling every rock and tree. We all stepped to the north side of the road to a shallow ditch as the 1970's white four door Ford LTD roared closer to our position. All four windows were down with elbows hanging out of each window. As the car approached I could see what looked like four young men with long hair driving slightly erratic, with the car swaying left and right from the middle of the road. The boy driving was Willie Dark, who, I was sure, did not have his license. As the car finally came even with us, it was obvious that the boys were up to no good. Willie had his head slightly tilted back, drinking out of a beer bottle and the passenger that was closest to us had some sort of home-made cigarette in his hand. It looked like the boys were in the back seat in a semi passed-out position. A billow of dust floated up over the top of our heads as each one of us almost simultaneously put our chins down and pulled our shirts up into our face to protect ourselves from the choking dust.

I could see enough through the dust to see Stewart throwing something at the car.

"Idiots, I'll break out your window!" Stewart yelled as his arm retracted from the throw. Soon everyone was brushing the dust off of their pants and shirt, not realizing that they were not making any progress in cleaning the muddy dirt-stained pants and shirts. Hey, in Penryn, it was cool to wear the pants a few times before putting them in the wash; that way it looked like you were a real country boy. Any boy that walked up to his friend's house with shiny new pants, shirt, or shoes, was automatically made fun of and called Mr. Clean. I once got a new pair of Levi jeans and threw them out on the dirt outside the garage next to the fireplace. I then proceeded to push the pants into the ground and grind them into the dirt. I then got Bear to grab them, and we played tug of war until they would rip a little. After that I knew my friends would not call me Mr. Clean.

After about five minutes of walking, talking, and shooting our BB guns at finches flying by, we finally reached the bend in the old dirt road that dipped down where the year-round brook was flowing through as old rusted drainage pipe under the dirt road. The sound of the water running over the rocks was getting closer and closer. The once open rocky pasture on each side of the road was now becoming a dark, dense wooded area surrounding the brook. The dogs were ahead of us already in the brook, frolicking and splashing around.

"Prepare arms men," Dwayne said in a low manly voice while pulling his BB gun up toward the road that lay ahead.

"What?" Stewart said with a chuckle.

"You heard what I said. We are now entering the Bickford forest. You never know what will be ahead. I have heard that mountain lions and bobcats roam this ranch."

"Where is the ranch house?" I asked in a quiet, timid voice.

"There is no ranch house," snapped Dwayne as he hurried his pace, putting him a few steps in front of us.

"Come here Zeke!" Ron yelled. Zeke did not respond but ran further away with Bear both of them nose down as if on a very important scent. Zeke was clearly not going to mind Ron.

Ron's voice cracked. "This is a little weird and too quiet."

"Ah, we're fine," replied Dwayne. "We have our BB guns to protect us. Keep them cocked and ready to shoot."

Now, Dwayne and the other boys had nice BB guns, but none compared to my new Crossman pellet gun. You see the pellet is cup shaped in the back so when the air from the gun is released it cannot escape around the pellet, so the full force of the air is used to push the pellet faster than a round bb. Ten to twelve pumps and the pellet will fly ten times faster than a BB. I felt safe as I was the only one with a pellet gun, which could easily penetrate the skin and muscle of an animal.

My Crossman pellet gun had a wooden pump that hung from the bottom of the barrel. "Poof, snap, poof snap, poof snap!" My gun was pumped up tight and ready to shoot if I had any problems. The three Penryn boys with guns were readying them like a bunch of soldiers ready for battle. It was late in the day and the afternoon sun was just beginning to move down in the west. There was not much talking going on now, just a bunch of boys looking ahead on the roadway in eager anticipation of finding the Bickford mines. We didn't know exactly where the mines were, but Dwayne was given a pretty good description of how to get there.

"It's in that direction!" Dwayne exclaimed, pointing the end of his BB gun toward an old steel gate about fifty yards away on the right side of the road. "That is were we leave the road to get to the caves."

Again, no one responded. All of us just peered down the road toward the gate, not changing the speed of our walk. Ron had a large canteen draped over his right shoulder. He carefully took it off his shoulder, unscrewed the small cap, and began to drink, not losing stride with us. Ron then passed it to me and then to the other boys. Soon everyone had a refreshing drink of water. I wiped the extra drops of water with my left arm off my cheek and chin.

Dwayne was the first one to reach the gate, with Stewart close behind. Owen was a good ten feet behind us walking in a gingerly fashion. Glenn was so slow I could never figure out how he could keep such a tall skinny frame. I rarely saw him run or act like he was in any hurry.

The gate was an old, pitted, bent-in rusted tubular cattle gate. The gate was riddled with 22 rifle bullet and shotgun pellet holes. The gate was locked up with an old, rusted chain that was wrapped around a greasy large railroad tie that stood solid as a rock. The railroad tie was the anchor for the old, rusted five-wire barbed-wire fence. The old rusted fence looked like it had not been repaired in decades.

Dwayne and Stewart pushed on the gate. There was a lot of play in it as the chain was too long and left a lot of room for someone to push the gate forward and step between the gate and the railroad tie. We only had to bend down a foot or so to go under the chain.

"Wait!" I exclaimed. "Look, there is a no trespassing sign. I don't know if we should go through."

Stewart shook his head. "What, can't you see that the old sign has been blown up and shot at by everyone that came up here?"

I guess he was right; the old metal sign was barely legible as it was riddled with so many bullet holes that it hung cock-eyed with old rusted bailing wire.

Owen finally caught up. "Hey I remember my brothers taking me up here when I was a little kid. I don't think we went through this way."

By this time Dwayne was already through to the other side. He turned around and peered angrily at Owen. "Well, I guess you need to be the one that needs to lead us to the caves then."

"Cool it, Dwayne, I just said that I don't remember this!" Owen exclaimed.

"Have you ever been to the caves, Owen?" Dwayne asked.

"Well, I...," Owen paused, bit his lower lip and looked at the ground. "I guess not."

Now Scott, standing in line to be the next one through the gate, paused.

"Dwayne, have you ever been to the caves?"

Now Dwayne looked a little more upset. "Well, no, but I have been this far with Slinkbell."

"Who?" Scott asked.

"Never mind, you'll meet him at school next week."

Each one of the boys proceeded to squeeze through the gate, the others waiting until all of us had reached the other side of the gate. The dogs were now nowhere to be found which caused me to become a little uneasy. They were our best protection.

"Well, we are all through. Now which way do we go Dwayne?" Stewart asked.

"I... well, I think we go... no, I am sure we just first follow the truck tracks in the grass."

It was clear that no one had driven past this gate in quite some time. The brownish, only slightly green grass had two distinct tire marks disappearing into the distant pasture. Dwayne and

Stewart were not paying attention, pointing their BB guns directly at Scott who was slightly in front of them.

"Hey, Dwayne," I exclaimed. "You might want to not shoot Scott in the back with your BB gun."

Without hesitation he and Stewart quickly lowered their guns so that they were pointing down, but they didn't turn around to acknowledge me. The area was absent of city sounds. The mild, windy conditions caused the leaves to rustle on the ground and branches to scrape together on the few big old oak trees in the pasture. The clearing that the tracks went through was only about seventy yards long until the pathway disappeared into a thick wooded area. The sun had continued to dip in the sky until it was now just hovering above the tops of the trees.   Scott stopped and turned to look at us behind him. "Hey, did anyone bring a flashlight?"

The look in everyone's eyes was the same: Everyone had the "Huh?" look.

Everyone stopped; what little dust was underfoot billowed up while everyone stopped and started patting their pockets. I could hear Dwayne snicker beside me. He reached into his right pocket and pulled out a small, red plastic flashlight.

Dwayne held up his flashlight high in the air. "Ok, dummies I thought of it. Did anyone else?"

I just remembered I had a small key ring in my pocket that had a little light attached to it. "I did." I held up the key ring with my little light that we could barely see.

I brought one," Ron replied, fiddling with his left side pocket. "I know it's in here; I put it there before we left, knowing that we were going to be looking at the inside of a cave."

Finally, after a few seconds of fiddling around, Ron brought out a very skinny three or four inch long mini-flash light.

Dwayne started to walk again, passing all of us just standing dumbfounded, wondering why we did not think of bringing a flashlight with us. Well, at least a good one.

Stewart piped up. "It was light out when we left, so I didn't think we would need a flashlight."

Dwayne, now a few steps in front of us, stopped in his tracks, turned to his left and looked back at Stewart. He furrowed his eye brows, opened his mouth slightly and began to shake his head slowly from left to right. "What?" Are you joking?"

Stewart shrugged his shoulders and pushed his lower lip forward and said "Well, yes."

Dwayne continued and we all followed closely behind. We were now only a few feet from the dense thicket of trees. I could hear the rushing of the water, and finally to my relief saw Zeke and Bear standing a few feet in front of us, completely wet.

Ron began to talk. "Ah, another ditch. Dwayne, is this the same ditch as the one that goes by the railroad tracks?"

"Yes, of course," Dwayne replied while not missing a stride.

The tire marks ended just before the ditch and a foot trail branched off from left to right along side the ditch.

"Which way," I asked.

Dwayne replied, nodding hid head to the left, and said "This way."

The already setting sun was now getting close to the horizon, but the dense trees made it seem like it was dusk. Though we did not yet need our two small flashlights and the one want-to-be flashlight, the dense-forest like canopy made it difficult to see. We walked single file.

The trees were almost all big old oaks, scrub oaks, and a variety of different shade trees. It was funny because we did not see a lot of cow pies in the area. It was evident that cattle had not been run in this area for quite some time. The odor was strong of sweet wild black berries and yet the smell of rotting flesh slightly overpowered the berries. The rotten smell became worse the farther we walked.

"What is that smell?" Scott asked while waiving his hand in front of his nose.

"Something dead I guess." Dwayne answered without stopping to pause.

"I think something died a long time ago and is probably bloating right now," Ron said.

Dwayne immediately replied, "Shut up, Ron, you don't know what it is."

"Yes, I heard stories from Steve Smith that when someone is killed, the dumping place for the dead bodies is at the Bickford Ranch. Come on, thousands of acres of wooded area? No one would find anyone."

"You could be right," Scott replied, "but the coyotes, bobcats and mountain lions would eat up a body pretty fast."

I checked to make sure everyone's BB guns were locked, cocked and ready to fire. The well-worn trail abruptly ended just into the large dense underbrush. An old, white two by six board crossed the ditch where it led to the continued trail on the steep mountain side of the ditch. We had been traveling on the west side of the ditch which was wide and stable. Now the trail was no more than two feet wide, and if you slipped off the edge you would plunge 100 or more feet to the bottom of a rock and tree filled valley. This was not safe as it was now almost dusk, and it was difficult to see in front if us without a flood flashlight.

Dwayne raised his light with his right hand. "Turn on your lights," he said, as he lowered his light and turned it on. Ron, who was in the back, turned his on. Surprisingly, Ron's light was real bright and lit up the way for at least three or four of us. My little key chain light seemed a little bit brighter now that it was starting to get dark.

The evening sounds were now upon us and I could hear the animals of the night. A screech owl was loudly proclaiming that he was near by. I could hear the howling of the coyotes down below us in the valley; there must have been at least a dozen of them. Their howls would be followed up with high pitched barking and whining. The howling did not seem to bother Zeke and Bear who were walking gingerly in front of me trying not to fall off the edge. However, the minute the coyotes began to bark and whine the dogs stopped, put their noses in the air and listened. I could see their tails dropping low, almost in-between their legs as if to say they were not sure if they were scared or not.

"Get going Bear," I said, trying to get her and Zeke to stay up with the rest of the boys. They continued on, trotting a little to catch up to the other boys. Ron and I hoofed it to stay up with the boys in front. I tripped slightly and caught myself from falling to the ground. The trail was generally well worn but a small rock or root would be sticking up every once in awhile, so it was important to watch your step so as not to fall off the trail and down into the valley.

Dwayne's light was shining up ahead and would bounce with every step. He was a good twenty feet in front of Stewart, Ron and me. Dwayne's light then turned sharply east and downward toward the valley. The light was steady so he obviously wasn't falling. As I approached, I could see the trail turned right from the ditch and started to zig zag down the mountain. I could hear small loose rocks falling below me, and Dwayne's light was moving farther and farther away. I turned behind me to face Ron.

"Let's pick it up guys. We are falling behind!" I increased my step to large jumping steps. I took a few of the steps down and then a few to the north and then south to stop me from traveling too fast down the steep hill. I continued to hurry down the hill but with some caution. We were finally making headway in catching Dwayne, but the light behind me was getting farther away the faster I went. I then heard a "Yelp" behind me. I knew then that Ron was okay and not far behind.

The bottom of the mountain did not seem so far away now as we were fast approaching it. Dwayne's flashlight had stopped and was now pointing back in our direction. The coyotes had stopped howling and the screech owl had silenced, clearly because we were making so much noise as we whisked down the hill.

As I reached the bottom, I saw Dwayne standing still with his right arm up in an "L" shape, moving his flashlight back and forth trying to find something. There were at least two separate trails, one going to the right and one going slightly center and left.

"Excuse me, dudes," Stewart said. He passed alongside each of us as we stood in a single file waiting for Dwayne to do something. Again, Bear and Zeke were off somewhere else. I believed they were off to the right as I heard the noise of something in the bushes. The sound then turned from just a rustling noise in the bushes to a quiet but distinct hissing sound much like a scared cat that I would hear late at night in the city that I came from. No one else seemed to be bothered so I ignored it.

Dwayne shined his flashlight down on the ground and turned his head slightly toward us. "I think the cave is this way," he said, raising his left arm and pointing to the trail slightly to the left of us.

"How do you know? You've never been here!" Scott exclaimed in a cracking, scared voice.

"Sinkbell told me how to get here, but I don't remember exactly which path to take once we get down to the bottom of the hill. I don't remember him saying anything about turning off the path once you go down the hill."

Stewart was now in front with Dwayne, stepping through the thick berry bushes to get around everyone else. Dwayne proceeded with his light pointing toward the now narrower vine, bush, berry, and tree lined path.

"Watch it!" Someone yelled in the front as a branch swung back toward me.

I grabbed it and pushed it out of my way with my right hand, causing the large oak branch to make a slight crack as I released it.

"Ahhhhh! Fred, tell me when you are going to hit me with a branch." Ron yelled.

"Sorry, I forgot." I replied.

I could now hear Zeke and Bear barking ahead and to the right of us in the general area that I heard the coyote sounds. The barking became more distant as we continued to travel down the less dangerous, flatter path.

"Bear, come here!" I yelled, not stopping so as to stay with the rest of the boys. I whistled loudly but the barking continued in a more panicked fashion. I could always tell when Bear found something because her bark went from a deep, every two second bark to a constant loud, whining bark. The pitch was clearly higher than her normal bark. It was obvious to me that she was excited about something. Zeke's bark was much deeper and distinct and was in a constant rhythm.

"Hey guys," I yelled. "Something's is wrong with the dogs!"

No one stopped or even gave a courtesy look; they just kept walking at a moderately fast steady pace. I was now behind everyone with only a little flashlight. By now all I could see was the perfect reflection of the sun just above the hills. It was now dusk and soon would be completely dark. Just then I heard Dwayne's voice in the distance.

"Here it is! I found it! It's here!"

We started to increase our speed to a full run. It didn't take much to pass Ron within a few yards. We rounded a sharp corner of the path that turned to the right back toward the area where we originally stopped. Within seconds we were up to Dwayne and Stewart. Dwayne was holding his flashlight upright, shining it toward a thicket of huge vines and blackberry bushes. Huffing and puffing, Ron showed up, his flashlight moving up and down frantically as he ran. He quickly pointed his light in the same direction of Dwayne's. His light was much brighter, and I could now distinctly see what looked like a cave some twenty five or so feet in front of us covered with large hanging grape-looking vines with large leaves. The vines were draped over a huge hole that was at least fifteen feet high by what looked like about ten feet wide. It was hard to tell for sure as the vines heavily covered the entrance.

Dwayne then shined his light to the right of the hole and I could see something metal in the bushes. Once Ron shined his light to the area, I could only make out one thing that was obviously an old, small mining car that I had seen in books.

The miners used the open cars to transport materials out of the mines. Ron now began to shine his light up and down and to the left and right like he could not make up his mind what he wanted to see. Dwayne's light turned from the car to a fixed position down on the ground in front of the big hole. There we saw two rusted, small railroad-type tracks going toward the large hole.

No one moved. We just kept following Dwayne and Ron's flashlights with our eyes. Of course, if you followed Ron's flashlight for too long you would get dizzy and fall down.

"Wow, man, look at that!" Someone yelled.

"Yeah, what a cool place," another boy replied.

At the time I wasn't sure who was talking, but I definitely agreed with them. Dwayne now shined his light on Stewart who was the only one that did not just stand there. He was already up to the opening of the huge mine and had started to move some of the vines away from the entrance with this hands.

"Stewart, wait a minute!" Scott exclaimed in an excited voice.

"Let's talk about this before we go in there."

"Talk about what?" Stewart said as he chuckled a little.

I could barely make out the image of Stewart without the flashlight. Dwayne turned his flashlight a little to the left of the cave and then back to the center of the cave. Stewart was gone, and I could see just a few vines moving left and right where Stewart had obviously walked in.

"Hey, someone bring a flashlight over here." Stewart's voice echoed, and he sounded like people in the movies when they talk in a big canyon or cave.

Ron stood next to me, stiff as a board. I looked at his light that was now pointing down at the ground. I could see Ron push the "Off" switch with his right thumb.

"Nah, nope, I aint' giving up this flashlight, and I'm for sure not going in there," Ron muttered quietly. Dwayne was the only one with a light, other than my small key chain light.

"Here you go," I shouted, throwing the keychain light at the front entrance of the cave. It landed in the "On" position right in front of the entrance, tangled up in the first layer of vines on the ground. Stewart's arm came out of the vines and grabbed it.

"Come on. It is pitch black in here," Stewart yelled.

I could hear Zeke and Bear barking, but now I was worried about what they might have found. I popped out of my awe inspired gaze of the cave when I heard one of the dogs yelp as if in pain.

"Bear, Zeke, come here, come here!" I yelled as I lifted my head from gazing at the entrance of the mine. The barking stopped and I could now hear them running down the trail, trampling through the bushes along the way.

As I turned back to the entrance of the cave, Dwayne and the others were just approaching the vines, and Dwayne was in the process of reaching out his right hand to brush away the vines. Within a few seconds Dwayne was in through the curtain of vines and then the others. Once Ron went in with his flashlight, it turned dark around me.

"Wait up guys, I can't see," I yelled, jogging up to the vines. I stopped and grabbed a few vines, parted them to the right and jetted through striking something and falling straight back on to the ground. As I lay on my back, I could see the lights going around in circles and shining above me on the top of the cave and then to the left side and to the right and then right in my eyes.

"Hey, what are you doing down there?" Ron asked in a curious voice.

"I don't know. I hit something," I replied as I put my right hand onto my forehead.

"Oh, watch out for that big beam that is falling from the ceiling," Ron stated.

As he was telling me this Ron shined his light on a huge six feet by six feet massive old beam that was obviously broken and hanging from the ceiling about five feet off the ground. I touched my forehead again and could now feel a welt starting to rise. "Ah, I've got a headache," I said.

Every word that was said and every move made echoed in the mine. It was very quiet and every little sound made sounded like a bomb going off.

I reached down with my right hand and sat up onto my butt. I slowly pushed myself up to the standing position, mumbling under my breath about how stupid that beam was.

Ron was nice enough to wait for me, but the other boys were at least fifteen to twenty feet in front of me. Ron shined his light on the walls that were shiny, and grey-black. They were rough cut and had clearly been chipped out with primitive tools. There were small piles of shale or rocks on the side of the cave where the rocks from the walls had fallen. The walls and ceiling were braced with large six feet by six feet and four feet by four feet wooden beams, most of which were hanging down from the ceiling or split and ready to collapse.

"Hey, Ron." I heard Dwayne say. Then, suddenly, "Watch out, bats!" He shouted suddenly, as a flurry of bats flew right above my head and to the right of me. All I could do was quickly duck and put my right arm and hand over my head. All I could see were objects above my head just briefly flying past the light from Ron's flashlight illuminating the ceiling.

As soon as the bats whisked by, the cave fell silent. Ron and I were together and the other boys were still a little bit ahead of us. However, the light that I saw from Dwayne's light was now becoming very dim. I wasn't sure if they were way down the tunnel or if his light was getting ready to go out.

"Ahh, what was that?" Stewart yelled.

I could now hear, down the cave, the sound of a rattlesnake.

"Rattlesnake! Don't move!" Someone yelled.

From the voices it was evident that the other boys were very close to Ron and me and that Dwayne's light was getting dimmer and dimmer.

"Ron, get down here with your light!" Dwayne yelled in an excited voice.

Ron hesitated and then slowly walked toward the other boy's voices. I followed close behind and within only a few feet we could make out two tunnels breaking off to the left and to the right of the main tunnel. The boys were all standing still in a huddle in the middle of what I would call the intersection of the different tunnels. Scott, Dwayne, Owen and Stewart were looking down to their left and right trying to find out where the snake was waiting to bite. Ron shined his light a foot or two to the right of the huddled boys where a large six by six beam lay on the ground. It was broken in half and was laying flat on the ground up against the corner of one of the walls. We could then see the snake who was harmlessly sitting coiled up behind the beam, not even able to strike any of us if he wanted.

All of the boy's eyes were now fixed on the rattlesnake that was safely behind the wooden beam.

"What do you think; that he is going to jump over the beam and bite you?" I exclaimed.

Slowly, everyone walked toward Stewart and me. Stewart reached down to pick up his BB gun that he had dropped in the excitement.

Dwayne's light was now almost completely out. All I could see was an orange glow from the lens.

Ron shined his light toward me. I motioned to the boys with my right hand. "Let's go. We need to get out of here before we have no light left."

It was funny. It felt like we were a mile underground when really we had only traveled no more than 100 feet into the cave. It was so pitch black that we could not see anything in front of us without a light. Within a matter of a minute or so we were out of the mine, standing in front of the vines. Bear and Zeke were both lying down, waiting for us to come out, too smart to venture into the dark old mine.

Pointing his flashlight toward the trail, Ron quietly and in a very polite way turned to us and said, "Well, let's get out of here before my flashlight goes out and our moms start to worry."

Chapter Eighteen
Back to the Mine

"The first day of school is Tuesday," Stewart whispered…and I want to go back and explore the cave."

"Shh, Stewart, they are saying the prayer," I said quietly as I turned toward him.

Mom was not tolerant of us boys talking in church, especially while the prayer was being said. Our family was sitting in our usual space, Mom in the pew next to the curtain and side entry door with the two youngest boys, David and Floyd, sitting right beside her. Dad never came to church but stayed home and worked on the ranch. Scott, Stewart and I sat behind her in the folding metal chairs leaning back just to the very point before we would fall over. Stewart's mom and dad were sitting alone in the middle pews up toward the front and never cared where Stewart sat. My mom always made us sit directly behind her in what we called the buffer zone between the chapel and the gym so she could keep a keen eye on us. If we did anything wrong, all she would say is that she was going to tell Dad and we would straighten right up. Dad always waited at home with the heavily knotted bamboo stick close to his seat just in case any of us acted up during church. People always asked Mom why we were so quiet in church. She never told them her secret weapon.

My eyes fixed on Stewart's during the prayer. I raised my eyebrows and nodded my head up and down. Scott also did the same, while keeping his arms folded and his head only slightly bowed. We were all dressed in nice pants, a white shirt and tie. This was the only time that Sister Toothly would not allow any hand-me-down clothes to be worn, so Stewart always looked nice and clean in church.

After prayer Bishop Thomas stood up at the pulpit which was a good seventy five feet from our position. He was a tall man with jet black, shiny hair that he combed straight back. He always wore either a black or dark blue coat with a string tie that had a Hawaiian emblem on the top. He began to speak. It was at that time that my attention focused away from him toward Scott and Stewart.

Scott was sitting on the far chair and leaned toward Stewart and me, looked to his left and right, then in a very quiet whisper-voice began to talk. "We need to go back to the mine tomorrow, before school starts."

"Tomorrow?" Stewart exclaimed with a slightly louder whisper. "Why not right after church?"

"Yeah, right." I exclaimed with disgust. I continued in a low voice. "No, let's go first thing in the morning so that we will not have to use our flash lights."

Stewart bobbed his head up and down, glancing back and forth between Scott and me.

"I'll tell the others." Stewart said.

The rest of Sunday couldn't have gone any slower as I was excited to get back to the Bickford Ranch mine.

The next morning I stood staring at the shoes on the rack in J.C Penneys.

"Come on Freddie. School is tomorrow and you need a new pair of shoes. Here are some good ones that say Converse on them. Aren't those the shoes that all the kids like?"

"Yeah, Mom, those are fine."

Monday had finally come and Mom had insisted in doing some last minute shopping. It was already 11:00 a.m. and school was starting tomorrow and today was our last day to get back up to Bickford Ranch before we got too busy with school. Everyone was waiting for Scott and me to get home to head back up to the mine. I swear mom made us try on every pair of shoes and every pair of pants in J.C. Penney. Then it was 11:45 and we were finally driving down Ridgeview Lane at about thirty mph, some twenty mph too fast for the narrow dusty roads. The dust billowed up behind the car, making it impossible to see out the back window.

I leaned over to Scott next to me in the back seat of the 1967 green Dodge station wagon. "I hope they haven't left without us."

"Don't worry they won't leave without us. Remember everyone but Dwayne was at church," Scott replied.

'Yeah, I guess your right."

Within a half hour after arriving home everyone was gathered around the tree in Ollis's forest where we had nailed down the first step for our future tree house.

We were soon on our way, this time armed with more flashlights. This time our route would be different; we would hop the fence next to the

Yelper house and trek down Allen Lane where we would eventually meet up with Owen at the corner of Allen Lane and Clark Tunnel Drive. Allen Lane was an old mill-maintained dusty dirt road that had many huge hills. This road would eventually ruin your car and would even cause you to wonder if a truck could make it up some of the hills in the winter.

Stewart was back to wearing his Levi jeans with red corduroy back pockets and a number of blue corduroy patches on the knee and lower right seat area.

"Why don't you have your mom sign those pants since she is the one that practically makes the pants from scratch?" Scott asked.

"Shut up, lips!"

Scott had a large oversized mouth and lips but this was the first time anyone had brought it up to him.

Scott turned to Stewart as they had just begun to crest one of the hills on Allen Lane.

"Okay, Tooth!"

I smiled as I walked and thought to myself: *Yes, maybe he was right, Stewart's two front teeth were clearly like rabbit's teeth. Maybe he got that as a curse from his dad killing all those cute little bunnies and eating them for lunch.*

Nothing else was said as we passed the very edge of Shepman's property that butted up against the edge of Allen Lane. I still marveled at how beautiful his property was: he owned the largest and most beautiful ranch in the immediate area.

Within a few minutes, we were greeting Owen at the corner of Allen Lane and Clark Tunnel.

Owen gasped. "It's about time! I've been sitting here forever!"

Owen was sitting in a small grassy area leaning up against the country road sign pole next to the road. He reached his right hand down flat on the ground and slowly got up from the ground.

"Let's go. We're burning daylight," he said.

This time it was much different: every boy had a flashlight. Everyone was there with the exception of Ron and every boy was armed with a BB gun. Of course Bear was tagging along as usual and seemed to love to sniff every bush and tree along the roadway. Bear was weaving back and forth and running ahead of us. She would then run back and forth again, clearly unnecessarily, running five miles during a two mile walk.

"Car!!" someone yelled out.

Everyone moved to the far right side of the old patched up blacktop road to let the car go buy.

"Whoosh." The wind from the vehicle blew my hair, and small pieces of gravel struck my back.

"The Dark boys again," Stewart said, mumbling something else under his breath.

I could see the old rusted white Ford pick-up getting smaller in the distance as it made a slight right and then left turn up the curvy road.

Dwayne shook his head and turned to us. "Where are they always going in such a rush?"

Scott chuckled. "Probably to check on their garden that they have planted at Bickford Ranch."

I was perplexed. "Huh? Why would they plant a garden all the way up there." I curiously asked.

Scott looked at me without missing a stride, smiled and just shook his head.

"You know," Dwayne exclaimed. "Like the one we saw in the woods by their house. They like to grow lots of plants and vegetables."

"Oh, is that what is in those two greenhouses next to their house?" Scott asked, sarcastically.

Stewart piped in. "Yeah, I saw those green houses one time. I was walking to Fred and Scott's house. What kind of vegetables do they grow in there?"

Scott chuckled again, "Boy, you guys are stupid!" Scott turned to Stewart.

"Now I see why you wear funny Levi pants and stupid patches all over them."

Stewart bent down, picked up a small rock and threw it at Scott. Scott only had enough time to lift his left leg up and try to block the rock with the side of his forearm. The small pebble-sized rock struck him in the side.

"Ouch! What is wrong with you, Tooth?" Scott stopped and paused as everyone continued to walk along the side of the steep road in single file. He yelled out "What do you think idiots? They're growing illegal plants and I think they are selling them. They are those little Japanese plants. I think they call them 'Bonsai'."

Scott took a few big strides to catch back up with us. "How do you know that?" Stewart asked.

"Well, you told me, Dwayne, that you saw Willie at school last year with a plant in a small container and he told you not to tell the teacher.

"Yeah, but I didn't say it was a Japanese plant. But it looked like one because it was held up with some small sticks."

"Probably so," Scott replied.

Everyone looked perplexed. Dwayne raised his hand slightly and without turning around exclaimed. "Just forget about it."

We were finally reaching the top of the steep, winding part of Clark Tunnel Road. I stopped to drink some good crisp clear Penryn water from my Boy Scout canteen. The longer that we lived in Penryn, the more we learned to be prepared, especially with lots of water. We never had to carry water with us when we were in the city, and if we carried a BB gun the police would tell us to take it home, advising us that some might mistake it for a real gun.

As soon as we arrived at the old steel gate we could hear some music playing down the road. It was distinctly Lynard Skynard and was muffled enough for us to not know exactly what song.

We each grabbed the top bar of the old iron gate and vaulted ourselves over, landing square onto the dusty two-tire marked road. No one hesitated; we did not want to be caught in the dark again. As we walked single file down the road, the sound of the music started to get fainter but the sound of voices became more prominent to our left. We had scarcely walked for five or ten minutes when Stewart, who was in the front, threw up his left hand high in the air to halt our walking. I almost ran into Scott who came to an abrupt stop. Now stopped, I could hear the voices up ahead and to the left. Stewart crouched down and waived his left arm in the downward position, holding it just a few feet off the ground.

"What is it?" Scott asked.

Stewart turned while still crouched. "I think it's the Dark boys and their friends," Stewart whispered.

Immediately my heart started to race: I could feel it pumping in my chest. Dwayne looked back toward me and had an unquestionably scared look on his face. While crouching, Dwayne waived both arms toward us to come together. I walked in the crouch position to Dwayne, meeting all the boys in the middle.

Stewart signed heavily, "I can barely see, but it looks like Willie Dark is sitting under that big oak tree over there in the pasture." Stewart sat up slightly and pointed with his left index finger toward a large heritage oak tree some seventy five yards away. We all lifted up slightly to take a look.

"There are more than just Willie. I see about four other guys," Dwayne replied with a cracking voice.

"Oh no!" I could not tell who said that, but as soon as I heard it I could see Bear trotting over toward the oak tree. I could then see smoke billowing up from the area Willie and his friends were sitting. There was a very slight rise and dip from our position to where Willie and his friends were. They were doing something because we could hear them laugh and could now see a lot of smoke billowing above them.

"Get down," Scott whispered in an excited voice. "Bear is going to give us away."

Everyone slumped immediately to the ground, flat and face first in the grass. We could hear the boys talking a little more loudly.

I heard "Get out of here!" Then I heard a yelp from Bear. Clearly she had been hit by something. Bear was now running toward our position and if she stopped she would just sit by us wagging her tail.

"Let's start scooting down the trail," Dwayne whispered. He immediately started to crawl using his stomach and arms to propel himself along the ground. We all started, looking like we were in a war zone trying to avoid bullets overhead. Bear was now only a few feet from us and we had to just hope that Willie and his group would not see the small billow of dust that we created by crawling.

Stewart stopped and turned his head toward the rest of us. We were now not in single file but in a tight three person formation, each trying to crawl away down the trail. The woods were only about fifty feet away but the noise from Willie and his friends did not seem to sound farther away. In fact, the sound from their voices shifted and I could hear Willie's distinctive voice belting out our way. It was obvious by the sound of their voices that they were looking our way.

I whispered, "Bear! Come here girl." Then, Bear was standing next to me, wagging her tail and walking along beside me as I was crawling. Bear looked to her left and then down toward me, hesitating and trying to figure out what to do. A whistle rang out from the oak tree. Bear refused to go and then suddenly a rock landed only fifteen feet from us.

"Bear come here," Willie yelled again. And then another different voice sounded out. "Bear, yeah, Bear, whatever, come here." This time the voice was more slurred and the person yelling was obviously drunk or having problems getting Bear's name out.

Stewart was the first one to reach the black berries next to the trail, and he slid around the corner to an even denser part of the trail. Within a matter of seconds we were all rounding the blackberries to our left, and we went into crouched running positions. Bear, as loyal as she was, continued to follow us. This, I said to myself, is the only time I wished that she was not so loyal. No matter where we stopped, she would give us away, so we had to keep running. The faster we ran, the faster Bear ran. I could hear the boys following down the trail behind us, calling "Bear" as she followed us. The trail was so heavily wooded and so sandy that I knew that they had no idea where we were. I stopped and then ran around a large scrub oak tree that was covered with blackberries and dense foliage. I had an idea: I grabbed the Tic Tacs that were in my pocket. Of course, Bear followed me directly behind the tree but had her tail was sticking out toward the trail. I quickly took a few tic tacs and threw them in the tall bushes right next to the tree.

I could hear the huffing and puffing of Willie and his friends coming up to my position. My heart was now really racing and I could swear any normal person could hear my heart thumping. My mouth was only opened very slightly so that I could take shallow, quick breaths. My exhale was slow and deliberate so that they could not hear me.

"Bear, what are you doing here?" Willie asked. I know Willie knew who Bear was because Bear had gone over to their house on a number of occasions and my dad had to go get her. I learned that was the way that country life was: everyone knew each others' dogs whether for goods reasons or bad.

Bear turned and looked at him, tail wagging the whole time. I could hear Willie's foot steps stomping down the foliage as he approached the tree. Bear looked back down where the Tic Tacs were. Then I had another idea: I shook the Tic Tacs in my hand quickly back and forth to imitate the sound of a rattlesnake.

I heard a quick high pitch screech from one of Willie's friends. "Rattlesnake! Ahhh!" I could hear the trampling of foliage as they scattered.

"Let's get out of here, run!" Willie shouted, his voice trailing off in the distance.

I waited for what seemed like forever but was actually no more than a minute, and then I came out from the back of the tree.

I stroked Bear on the top of the head as she stood looking at me with her tail wagging. "Good job, Bear, good job," I told her. Within a minute I caught up with the boys who were quietly walking along the deep forested path.

"There has got to be another easier way to get to that cave!" Dwayne exclaimed.

Stewart sighed, "Yeah, didn't we go another way last time?"

Dwayne stopped and turned back toward us. I was breathing a little bit harder than the other boys, still reeling from my run to catch up with the group.

"Yeah, but we didn't have Willie Dark and his thugs chasing us, did we?" Dwayne replied.

"Look, there is a trail going down the hill!" Scott exclaimed while pointing his right index finger toward the right side of the hill. The trail went almost straight down the hill with an occasional left and right turn. It was only about 100 feet down to the valley floor and seemed like running might be a better option then walking all the way around the mountain.

"Whoopee!" Scott yelled as he pushed Stewart and Dwayne to the side and immediately started running down the hill, leaning back and sort of jumping as he ran down. The run was definitely a half out-of-control run, but clearly not something dangerous that Mom wouldn't want to see us doing. Soon everyone was following, including Bear. I was the last one to head down the hill, and I felt small rocks being kicked on me by Bear who was directly behind me. A small clearing in the dense underground appeared at the bottom of the hill. Everyone came to a halt as the steep trail ended at the bottom of the hill.

"The cave's over there." Stewart pointed toward an open area of the valley.

"I see it," Dwayne said.

"I see it also," Scott responded.

Soon we were all in a full run to try to get to the mine first. This time the sun was just starting to drop in the sky when everyone arrived at the entrance to the vine covered cave.

This time there was no hesitation! Stewart was first. "Ready? Lights on?"

Everyone switched their lights on. Scott, Stewart, Dwayne, Owen and I were more prepared this time. Dwayne pushed away the thick vines from the entrance with his left hand and started into the dark cave. Nothing had changed except now that we had more light, there was much more to see.

I pointed my bright light down and could see very large paw prints that were obviously from a mountain lion. Up against the west wall, not far from the entrance, were some animal remains that looked like that of a smaller animal such as a small sheep or goat. Maybe this was what we smelled last time. Everyone was walking a little bit faster this time to get into the mine.

"Watch out for the beam!" Scott exclaimed, pointing his light just in front of me and overhead.

"I know. I hit it last time." I replied.

The lights were moving all around the rock tunnel. I could now see sparkles of silver and gold in the wet granite rock. I could now clearly see that the walls and ceiling were damp from seeping water, making them sparkle and shimmer more than a normal dry rock. The mine echoed every time someone hit something or said anything.

"Which way do you want to go?" Dwayne asked.

Dwayne was standing at the intersection where three different tunnels branched off in three different directions. Everyone was shining his light into the tunnel. The tunnels looked like they were the exact same size and looked to be very long. The railroad tracks on the ground split and went down each tunnel. You could see on the ground where an old switch was with the handle being long gone, and a hole with a small, stagnant, rusty pool of water sitting in it.

"Let's break up," I suggested in a bold manner.

"I don't know about that," Owen replied, shining his flashlight in my face.

Just as Scott finished, Stewart started to walk off to the left tunnel. "I'm going this way if anyone wants to come with me. Let's go."

"Remember, Scout's rule, always have a buddy," Scott said, laughing, and starting to follow Stewart.

Owen and I started to walk down the tunnel to the right, assuming that Dwayne would follow. Owen gathered closer to me than he had before. "Not so close," I snapped at Owen.

"Hey, where is Dwayne?" Owen asked.

"I don't know," I replied, turning my light back behind us.

"Turn your light off." Owen and I turned our lights off and I could see a light coming from the middle tunnel. Dwayne obviously went off on his own down the middle tunnel.

"Should we follow him?" Dwayne asked.

"No, let's go down here a little way and see what is down here."

We broke the cardinal rule in letting Dwayne go down a tunnel by himself. After only a few feet I noticed smaller tunnels branching off of the main tunnel that we were now on. These tunnels were about half the size of the main tunnel and had no tracks leading into them. The most bazaar and spooky thing, though, was the fact that each one of these tunnels were no longer than twenty to thirty feet before water started to appear. After passing a few of these small tunnels, I decided that we needed to explore one of them even further.

"Owen, let's take this tunnel," I said. "Yeah, so we can get lost?" he said. "What are you going to leave on the ground so that we can find our way back?"

"Ah, nothing, we won't get lost." I replied.

"Okay!" Owen exclaimed, "You first."

I turned to my left, shining my flashlight into the tunnel that was no bigger than five feet wide and six feet high. The ground was a little damper and began sticking to our shoes. The tunnel made a slight turn to the left and my flashlight caught something that reflected back.

"Water," Owen stated.

"Yeah, and lots of it." I added.

We both shined our flashlights toward the back side of a tunnel that opened up into a small room about twenty feet wide by about eight feet high. There was something like a beach at the edge of the water. It was an underground lake with a small beach, with the beach portion of the underground lake made up of larger pebbled rocks mixed with some light-brown decomposed granite. As we approached, the lights shined on crystal clear water that looked clear, cool, and crisp. I had never seen water so pure and clean looking in my life. There were some footprints where an obviously large man had walked in the beach area. I could not tell how old they were or how long they had been there. It was obviously from a work boot, though, not a tennis shoe.

"Wow, would you look at that water." Owen remarked.

"Yeah," I answered. "I think this water must be from some underground spring."

Owen bent down, set his flashlight next to the water, and put his right hand in a cupping position and scooped up some water.

"Don't drink that, you idiot! You don't know what is in this water." I said.

"Yeah, but I'm thirsty," Owen replied.

"Up to you, but I wouldn't touch that. Here is some of my water."

I handed Owen my Boy Scout canteen. "Don't drink it all; just take sips." I reminded him.

"Okay." Owen proceeded to unscrew the white cap off of the canteen that was attached with a thin silver chain. The water dripped down his chin as he tilted the canteen back, gulping down water like he had not taken a drink in days.

"Hey, enough!" I snapped, grabbing the canteen away from him. I put the cap back on, put the canteen strap around my neck, and started cocking my BB gun.

"Let's shoot into the water and see what happens," I said. I carefully twisted my gun right and left with the small action open. A BB slipped into the small round chamber. I closed the bolt action portion of the gun and aimed at the water.

"Pop!" The water splashed a little where the BB penetrated.

"Well that was real fun," Owen laughed quietly. Owen then started to walk over to the far right side of the beach and continued to point his light into the water.

"Pop!" I shot another BB into the water. Owen muttered quietly, "Hey look at this."

"What?"

I started to walk toward Owen who was only five or ten feet from my position. It was then that I noticed Owen holding his flashlight in his right hand at head level in front of him. He was pointing the flashlight in the downward position toward the back of the tunnel. I focused my light on the same area. I could see something brown and red, some sort of box. I leaned further over the water with the light now penetrating better through the water. I could barely make out some writing on it. The small rectangular box was no more than six or eight inches high by about two feet long. It had some rusted type of straps on it. The problem was that it was in about three or four feet of water and it was toward the back of the large cavernous part of the cave. It was at least forty feet away.

"Let's go get it," Owen said.

"Okay, go ahead." I replied.

"Oh, I meant you go get it and I will hold the light."

I raised both arms in the air. "Sure, why not!" I put my gun down, handed the light to Owen, and sat down on the beach area. I carefully took my shoes and socks off. I could hear Bear barking in the distance; she must have been with Scott and

Stewart. Other than that distant noise, there was a complete eerie silence in the tunnels. As I took my shoes and socks off, I was taken aback at how this tunnel was once a thriving place with mine workers busily breaking rock away from the walls, drilling shafts, blowing up walls, all to find just a few ounces of gold. I could only imagine the hard work and simple lives that these miners lived. A life underground in the dark would not be one that would be very desirable.

"Come on, hurry up!" Owen squawked. "What are you doing, day dreamin'?"

I stood up, rolled up my pants to the bottom part of my knees, and slowly put my right foot into the water.

"Yow! That is cold!" I said.

"Okay, just don't think about it," Owen said.

I was not in the water more than ten seconds when I noticed a cloud of gray and brown dirt billowing up from my feet and clouding up a two foot radius around me. Owen grabbed my left arm. "Whoa, wait a minute dude, get out." Owen's grip on the back of my left upper arm was now tightening. "If you try to walk out there, you will see nothing and never be able to get that box."

"Yeah, you're right," I replied. I slowly stepped back with my right foot out of the water. The dirt cloud was now about three feet in diameter and was starting to slowly settle.

"You're going to have to swim for it, Fred."

"Swim? I'll freeze to death!"

Owen walked over to the water, bent down from the waist and swished the water with his hand.

"Ah, it's not too cold. I almost took a drink of that water."

I could see Owen's hand was bright red from having his hand in the cold water for only a few seconds. Owen immediately put his hand in his right pocket to warm it up.

"Okay, I'll have to swim over there to the box and grab it," I agreed. I did not hesitate, for those who hesitate chicken out, I thought.

"Splash!" I jumped into the water like a dog, chest first, head up, and started to immediately dog paddle. I had never in my life experienced water that cold. My head started to shake and my teeth chatter. My fingers became instantly numb.

"It's just ahead of you and to the right," Owen stated. Owen's flashlight was beaming in an area right in front of me.

I could barely hear him as my ears were ringing with the cold. I swam faster. After what seemed like an hour I arched back slightly and started to tread water. "Where is it?" I yelled.

"Just below you and to the right."

Knowing I was close, I looked down and could see the box right where Owen told me. I quickly arched back even more and placed my feet down. The water was up to my chest. Dirt immediately started to billow up and just before it began to engulf the box, I reached down with my right hand, leaning far enough to get my face wet, and grabbed the open box. It was heavy and I pulled it up, holding tightly onto the side.

"I've got it!" I shouted in excitement. I quickly turned and walked as fast as I could toward the beach area. I could feel my feet sinking down in the muddy bottom. I was now numb and I could not even feel the cold water. I reached with my left hand to hold the box on the bottom and with my right hand gently held the side of the box. I stepped out of the water when I reached the beach, feeling the cold mine air on my wet body.

"Would you look at that!" Owen exclaimed while bending slightly and pointing his bright flashlight directly at the box. I bent down and picked up my flashlight from the ground and turned it on.

"Dynamite! Newmont Mining Corp.!" Owen read.

The box had one old wet stick of dynamite still sitting in it, leaned up against the inside of the box. It would not move and was obviously stuck. It was in perfect condition and looked as if someone had just placed the box down a few days ago. I touched the dynamite stick with my index finger and the red outside of the dynamite stick collapsed, leaving a dark-red mark on my finger.

"Careful, that stuff is real delicate." Owen exclaimed.

"Ok, I won't touch it. That must have been the name of the company that owned the mine." I bent down and swished the water in and out of the box until the stick of dynamite loosened and floated out of the box. The stick was so old it turned into dirt and just floated away when the box was shaken.

"Let's go, I'm getting cold," I said. By this time I was shaking more vigorously.

"Okie dokie," Owen replied, throwing my gun over his shoulder.

"Now which way did we come from?" I asked.

"We came from the left," Owen replied in a gleeful tone. Owen led the way as I skipped on one leg trying to put my shoe on the other foot.

"Hey, wait up Owen!" I yelled as I continued to hop on one foot while at the same time attempting to put on my dry, black converse high tops.

Owen was just about to the edge of the open area where the tunnel began when we heard a loud scream that sounded like it was coming out of the tunnel. The scream echoed over and over again.

My second shoe was finally on and I could start to move quicker. Bear was now next to my feet, pestering me by getting in front of my every step. It was as if she knew something exciting was going on. Within a few seconds, flashlights in tow, Owen and I turned right out of the small open tunnel into the secondary tunnel Owen and I had earlier traversed. We could now hear louder screams. The screams caused a tingling to go up and down my spine. We were now at an almost full run, careful not to trip over the railroad tracks. I could see a flashlight beam coming from the tunnel up ahead to our right, the light bobbing up and down as if someone was running.

"Aaah, run!" someone screamed from the tunnel.

The light drew closer to the intersection of the tunnels. I could also see a light coming from the tunnel directly across from us, and I heard another yell, now louder.

"Aaah, no, no, get out of here!" Then I saw Dwayne coming out into the intersection area where Owen and I were now standing, slightly bent over catching our breath.

Dwayne's light was on the ground and I could see the silhouette of his face, sweating and looking like he had just seen a ghost.

"What is it, Dwayne, have you gone crazy?" Owen asked.

By this time Scott and Stewart were standing to the left of us, huffing and puffing, flashlights pointing directly at Dwayne. I could now see Dwayne better, and his face was flushed with red on his cheeks and pure white around the rest of his face. He was wet from about his chest area down and his shoes were covered in mud.

After a few seconds Dwayne caught his breath, straightened his body up halfway, and then shrugged his shoulders. He lifted and pointed his right arm toward the direction that he had just come out of the tunnel. "I just saw a dead man floating in the water down there!"

Owen immediately yelled, "What?"

Stewart stepped forward pointing his light closer to Dwayne's face. "Huh? A dead man? Are you sure?"

Dwayne continued. "I swear, the end of the tunnel is flooded and I thought that I saw something submerged only a few inches under the water up against the wall in the tunnel." Dwayne paused. "I just know I walked into the water and it started to get all cloudy and muddy and when I got to the object and grabbed it, it had legs and bumped up against me. I saw what looked like a face under the cloudy water, and then the body floated down and away from me."

"What did it look like?" I asked.

"I don't know. It had a checked long sleeved shirt and I did not try to look at it any more before I ran."

Everyone paused and nothing was said for at least ten seconds or so. No one knew what to say. Stewart pointed his flashlight toward the end of the tunnel that Dwayne just came from. The rest of the lights were still focused on Dwayne's face. I asked myself if this was just a joke that Dwayne was pulling on us.

"Well, let's go and see what it is," Stewart said as he started to walk carefully down the tunnel. No one followed, but just stood there looking at Dwayne. Bear started to follow Stewart down the tunnel.

Scott turned his flashlight toward the tunnel and started to gingerly walk down it as well. "Okay, let's go."

Soon everyone's lights were pointed toward the tunnel with no one walking with any haste, Owen leaned over to me as he took one slow step after another. "What do you think it is?"

"I don't know, but I don't think he was kidding. Remember Steve Smith telling us that the caves are where the dead bodies are hidden?"

"No, I don't remember him telling me that." Owen replied.

Unlike the tunnel that Owen and I had been in, this tunnel just ended in water and there was no beach to speak of. Shining my light up and around and then down on the ground, I could see the old rusted tracks disappearing into water. The rest of the boys were stopped looking out into the water with their flashlights. As I approached I focused my light in the area that all the other boys were looking at. The water was thick and clouded with dirt that had been obviously stirred up from Dwayne.

Stewart nodded his head up and down. "Well, I know you weren't kidding, but you stirred up all the dirt, and now we can't see anything." The tunnel was very long and filled with water and probably over five feet deep in places.

I could then see where Dwayne's wet footprints had come out of the water, but there was nothing anyone could see in the murky water. We all continued to lean slightly over the water, moving our lights slowly over the top to see if we could see anything.

"Nothing, I see nothing," Scott replied in a quiet voice.

"Splash, splash." Sure enough, Bear was now wading in the water, continuing to stir up the dirt on the bottom so that now all we could see was dark brown water.

"Bear get out of there," Scott yelled with a deep growl in his voice.

Bear paused, turned around from her dog paddle, and soon was shaking the water off of herself, right next to us, getting the lower part of our pants wet.

"I swear it was in there; I felt it and saw it." Dwayne exclaimed.

"Was your light on Dwayne?" Scott asked.

"Shut up, of course it was, I could see that it was a body."

"It looks a little dim to me," Scott replied.

Stewart did not hesitate but walked right into the murky brown water. All of our flashlights were focused on him. Once the water reached his lower stomach he rose up and gasped "Ohhh, that is cold! A dead body could stay in good shape for a long time in this water."

Stewart immediately turned around and came out of the water. He stood there dripping wet, standing just on the edge of the dry ground. "Man that is cold! I ain't going in there again."

No one said anything but just kept shining their lights toward the murky water.

Dwayne whispered as if talking to himself. "I swear I saw a dead man and touched him; I don't care what you guys say."

Scott turned his flashlight toward the tunnel. "Let's get out of here. It's getting late."

"Yeah, let's go! That body has probably been there a long time." Owen stated.

One by one each boy turned and started to gingerly walk back down the tunnel, almost in an army-like orderly fashion. No one was speaking;

you could have heard a pin drop if it wasn't for Bear running back and forth, climbing over piles of dirt and wooden beams.

No more than ten minutes had passed when we saw very dim daylight shining through the hanging ivy vines. Owen was the first one to walk through the vines and out of the mine. It was dusk and all we could see was an orange glow on the horizon. Within seconds, everyone was outside of the mine, saying nothing.

We slowly marched up the hill toward the top. Again no one wanted to talk much as we all were thinking the same thing: *Was there really a dead body in there?*

Owen finally broke the silence. "Well, it sure is beautiful up here, dead body or not!

"Yeah, and it was a great summer, but school starts tomorrow!" Stewart replied from behind Owen.

"But what about the dead guy? Should we tell the police?" Scott asked in a very hushed tone.

"No, Scott, I don't want them to think that we had anything to do with it," Dwayne replied.

"Do with it? We didn't do anything wrong," Scott snapped.

"Well," Dwayne said, "I don't know about you, but I am going to forget about it. That body is so old that probably whoever it is has been long forgotten."

"Well...good idea, I guess. But one thing for sure, the rumors were right: Bickford Ranch has a cool mine with hidden secrets," Scott proudly stated.

"Shouldn't we come back after the dirt has settled?" I asked.

"No way," Owen blurted out. "Leave good enough alone. I don't want any trouble!"

Maybe there really was a body, or maybe Dwayne was really just putting us on. I really didn't care at that point. The stars were just starting to come out in the sky and already they were as bright as I had ever seen. There were no lights and no other people even close to this area to ruin the beautiful view. There were also no street lights, honking cars, neighbors making loud noises, or dogs barking. "Man, I said, what a beautiful night. Look how bright the stars are! I never saw the stars so bright in Sacramento."

At that instant I remembered something important, "Hey, you guys, at least we get to see that babe Valerie Smith at school tomorrow!

Stewart chuckled from behind me, "Yeah, ask the teacher if you can sit next to her in class. There will probably be a lot of guys waiting in line!"

"Oh, I'll just take my chances," I replied, and then I looked at the dynamite box in my hand. "Anyway, I've got a cool box that I'm going to put in my room. I wonder how old it really is?

"That thing could be close to 70 years old ," my older brother replied, "But I know one thing—don't let Dad know where you got it! Not unless you want your butt beaten."

Dwayne raised both arms into the air, fists clinched. "Isn't this a great place to live? What a summer, what a summer!"

"Yeah, who would have thought," Scott said nodding his head up and down.

Epilogue
Book One

So ended the first summer that we, the Nickel boys, lived in Penryn. Many of the neighboring Penryn boys that we met and had adventures with that summer would remain good friends well into the future, and the adventures we had during the summer of '73 were only a beginning of much more fun to come.

Next book, *The Penryn Boys: School Days of 1973-1974.*

ABOUT THE AUTHOR

Frederick W. Penney is the author of Penryn Boys. All his life Frederick wanted to write a series of novels about boys growing up in a small rural town like Penryn, California. Frederick has always believed that one should not focus on the author, that such focus takes away from a good book. Frederick could have been a Penryn Boy or may have grown up in Ione, Idaho or Richburg, South Carolina or somewhere near you. It does not matter.

Fortunately, Frederick has had some interaction throughout his life with real Penryn Boys, a breed of boys not found anywhere on earth. Whether this book is based on true life stories of Penryn Boys does not matter as there are small towns all over the United States where boys and girls had similar experiences to those of the Penryn Boys. Frederick loves the simpler times where boys and girls were free from the ills of society, the fears of the big city and where it was not bad to be a little naive about life.

This picture depicts an example of true Penryn Boys, one may be a picture of Frederick as a young man or this might just be pictures of real life Penryn Boys. Again, it does not matter. Who is Frederick Penney? Who cares, it does not matter.

FREDERICK W. PENNEY

A Pennco Publishing Book

PENRYN BOYS
CUSTOM JEANS

NAME_____

ADDRESS_____
_____

CITY: _____STATE: _____ZIP:_____

TELEPHONE NUMBER: _____

E-MAIL ADDRESS_____

I AM IN INTERESTED IN:

☐ PENRYN BOYS JEANS

☐ PENRYN GIRLS JEANS

☐ OTHER

PLEASE VISIT THE PENRYN BOYS WEBSITE AT

WWW. PENRYNBOYS. COM

FOR MORE INFORMATION AND ORDERING YOUR
OWN CUSTOM JEANS.

MAILING ADDRESS
P. O. BOX 7
LOOMIS, CA 95650